Praise for *Growing Up With G.I. Joe's*

"Janna, I am so glad that you told the G.I. Joe's story. You got it right!"

I. Joe's
CEO, 1976–1992  –1998

*"In the early decades after Wor. 's,
Fred Meyer and Tom Peterson p........... .... strategies
in the Pacific Northwest. This personal account is a worthy addition to
the history of that creative era before the arrival of the major chains."*

—Fred Leeson
Author of *My-Te-Fine Merchant, Fred Meyer's Retail Revolution*

*"Ed Orkney was raised during the Great Depression in the timber
community of Hoquiam, Washington. The ingenuity and self
confidence he gained at an early age turned G.I. Joe's into one of the
largest retailers in the Pacific Northwest. An inspiring story!"*

—Tom Quigg, business owner and creator of
The Harbor—A Culture of Success, www.CultureofSuccess.com,
Listing notable residents of Grays Harbor County, Washington

*"The story of this family business is also the story of Portland,
intertwined with the Vanport Flood, suburbanization, and the
transformation of a provincial city into a metropolis."*

—Carl Abbott, Portland State University,
Author of *Portland in Three Centuries*

*"A great look at the founder of G.I. Joe's, Ed Orkney, his family, and
the early days of the store. The book continues the G.I. Joe's story after
Ed Orkney's passing to the end of the business in 2009."*

—Ron Menconi, G.I. Joe's and Joe's Sports, Outdoor and More,
Sr. Vice President, 1999–2009;
National Sporting Goods Association (NSGA),
Chairman, 2003–2004

"In the early 1950s, while shopping for cartons of Pall Mall cigarettes for Mom, Dad discovered a treasure in North Portland—G.I. Joe's! Thereafter he took us there every Saturday morning, originally to the old tent structure, then later to the wooden store with the parking lot surrounded by empty bombs. It was a kid's dream. For the next 60 years, I spent way too much of my time (and money) at G.I. Joe's. I always felt at home there. Thank you Ed Orkney for being such a big part of my life!"

—Jack Mattice, Hospital Consultant,
Member, Coastal Conservation Association Pacific Northwest
(CCA PNW)

"We listened and followed our northwest communities."
—Ed Ariniello, G.I. Joe's, and Joe's Sports, Outdoor and More
Vice President, Operations, 1998–2009

"This book is a tribute not only to the Ed Orkney family and G.I. Joe's but to all other free-wheeling entrepreneurs who pioneered retail in the Pacific Northwest. We are proud to be part of their history."
—Mark Williams,
Worldwide Distributors, President

Growing Up with G.I. Joe's

*From war surplus store in a tent
to multi-million dollar retail chain—
how my father, Ed Orkney, built G.I. Joe's*

By Janna Orkney

Columbia Press

Portions of this book have appeared in a slightly different form in a blog by the author, **www.growingupwithgijoes.blogspot.com**, from 2008 to 2012.

The author is grateful for permission to quote from the 50th Anniversary edition, dated February 23, 2005, of the newsletter of Worldwide Distributors, based in Kent, WA.

The author thanks publisher, SportsOneSource, LLC, for permission to publish photos from the December 1973 issue of The Sporting Goods Retailer, from an article titled, "Spawned in Tent, Oregonian to Chalk up $4 Million in '73."

Printed in the United States of America

Library of Congress Control Number: 2014921235

ISBN: 978-0-9891131-0-6

Publisher's Cataloging-in-Publication *(Provided by Quality Books, Inc.)*

Orkney, Janna.
    Growing up with G.I. Joe's : from war surplus store in a tent to multi-million dollar retail chain : how my father, Ed Orkney, built G.I. Joe's / by Janna Orkney.
    pages cm
    Includes bibliographical references and index.
    LCCN 2014921235
    ISBN 978-0-9891131-0-6

    1. G.I. Joe's (Firm)--History. 2. Army-Navy stores--Northwest, Pacific--History. 3. Chain stores--Northwest, Pacific--History. 4. Orkney, Ed, 1915-1976. 5. Orkney, Janna--Family. 6. Businessmen--United States --Biography.   I. Title.

HF5482.5.O75 2015   381'.1906579549
                          QBI14-600203

Book design by Susan L. Wells

For my three children, Jamil, Sam, and Laurie,

and for all the children who had such fun

going to G.I. Joe's to look for treasures,

especially in the early days.

Contents

Growing Up
with G.I. Joe's

Prologue

The early years of G.I. Joe's happened in a special time and place. The time was special because it was the decade after World War II, when Americans were full of dreams and energy, working to build prosperous lives for themselves after the years of fighting and sacrifice.

The special place where G.I. Joe's was located was Portland, Oregon, in the center of the Pacific Northwest, just across the Columbia River from Vancouver, Washington. There in the middle of the twentieth century, perhaps residents lived more in tune with the rhythms of nature than folks did in most other places in America. After all, it had been less than a century since large numbers of pioneers settled in the region. The Tribal People were still fishing in the old ways on the Columbia, and magnificent old growth forests abounded.

And just like the time and place, early G.I. Joe's was special. Folks loved to shop there, looking for the latest items for sale. A lot of the merchandise in the store was bought by my father, Ed Orkney, at government auctions of military merchandise left over from the war. And the auction merchandise that he bought was always changing, which meant that customers never knew what wonderful new items they would find in G.I. Joe's sales bins and shelves.

Dad continued building the business while I was growing up. By the time he died in 1976, G.I. Joe's had expanded from one small war surplus store in a tent into a chain of six large general merchandise stores in Portland and one in Salem, Oregon.

I continue the story of G.I. Joe's growth throughout the Pacific Northwest in the following decades. That includes the business buyout by California investors in 2007 and then its bankruptcy and liquidation under the new name, Joe's Sports, Outdoor and More, in 2009.

Yes, the 31 stores in the chain closed doors in 2009, but it could be said that the last two years of the business were out of sync with the preceding 55 years. Until 2007, the G.I. Joe's story was about the long-term, conservative expansion of a homegrown business that resonated with customers. The merchandise mix may have changed, but it was always compelling.

I want to share this story with you because the history of G.I. Joe's was interwoven with the history of the Pacific Northwest for almost six decades. And, if you live in the region, this history might be part of your own personal story, too.

If you live elsewhere, you may have visited war surplus stores similar to G.I. Joe's in the early days and might have similar stories to tell like those that appear in these pages. Or, this history may remind you of family tales about your father, grandfather, or even great grandfather returning from serving in World War II and building a new life in a way that still matters to descendents today.

While *Growing Up With G.I. Joe's* is the unique account of my father and mother and the family business, it can also be looked at as a tribute to all the folks of my parents' generation. These men and women persevered through all kinds of hardships and challenges during the Great Depression and World War II. And when peace came, most of them moved forward with hope and vision, just like my parents did.

I salute them! ▪

Definitions

G.I.   Initials standing for Government Issue, such as clothing and equipment issued to U.S. military personnel

G.I. Joe   A nickname for a member of the United States armed services in World War II

Clarifications

Army Air Forces   The aviation branch of the United States armed forces during World War II. Originally the Army Air Corps, the name change to Army Air Forces occurred in 1941. War locations or theaters in World War II were served by different Army Air Forces. For example, Ed Orkney was stationed in New Guinea in 1943 and 1944 as part of the Fifth Army Air Force serving in the South West Pacific Theater.

In 1947 there was another name change for the aviation branch of the United States armed services, and the Army Air Forces became the Air Force.

G.I. Joe's   A war surplus store located in Portland, Oregon, which Ed Orkney owned in partnership with five others in 1948. Orkney bought the business in 1952 and became the sole owner. G.I. Joe's grew to become a chain of big box retail stores throughout the Pacific Northwest.

Chapter 1

And Store Makes Five

David and I sit on front porch of our home
near Portland, Oregon, in the summer of 1951.

When I was growing up, it was like there were five members in my family. There was Mom, Dad, my brother and I, and "the store." My mother was Charmian Orkney and my father was Edward Orkney; my brother was David, also known as Corky, and I was Jan. The store was G.I. Joe's, a small war surplus store in a G.I. hospital tent in Portland, Oregon, that my father bought in 1952.

As time passed, the original store building changed from a tent with siding of horizontal wooden boards, to a conventional wood frame building, to the last building addition of concrete walls and a wood and composite roof. And G.I. Joe's grew from one small structure to three large buildings next to each other in North Portland. Before Dad died in 1976, G.I. Joe's had expanded with three big box stores in additional locations in the Portland area and another one in Salem, Oregon.

Eventually, G.I. Joe's, with a name change, grew to include 31 stores located in Oregon, Washington, and Idaho, with control of the chain passing from my family in 1998. In 2007, the chain was bought by a California investment firm that changed the store's name, conducted rapid expansion and led the business into bankruptcy and liquidation in 2009.

However, the swift ending to the former family business does not dim its success in the 57 preceding years, or the hard work and creativity that made the store such an integral part of life in the Pacific Northwest. That is what I focus on in this book.

And I look at how, before and after Dad's passing, store locations were added, the G.I. Joe's merchandise mix was often modified to compete in changing times, and peripheral stores were opened and closed or were sold.

In 1960, when there was still only one large G.I. Joe's in North Portland, Dad experimented by opening a small shoe store in a mall in the Portland-area city of Milwaukie. I worked there one summer during high school, and then the store closed soon after.

There was also the Jean Machine chain started by my brother in the mid-1970s that sold jeans and tops to teenagers and young adults. The first Jean Machine was located in front of the original North Portland G.I. Joe's store and connected to it, replacing a Levis-only shop that David had also developed. Jean

The Rockwood store opened in 1970 in an area east of Portland that became part of the City of Gresham in the mid-1980s. It was the first branch store.

Machine thrived because teens loved to shop there. By 1983 the chain included at least 15 stores in cities ranging from Olympia, Washington, to the north, to Eugene, Oregon, to the south. Then in the early 1980s, management started the Action Outfitters chain that sold upscale athletic shoes and clothing in three Portland area locations.

Finally, total focus was brought back to G.I. Joe's to make it the best store it could be, without the distraction of other store concepts. Management closed Action Outfitters, and the Jean Machine chain was sold.

I don't believe in the beginning, that my father could have ever envisioned all the stores and merchandise variety and locations that would develop for G.I. Joe's. And I don't believe he could have foreseen all the talented and diverse people that would join in building the business over the years.

However, before Dad ever had a store, he did know what he wanted to do with his life. He wanted to buy and sell merchandise and that was how he started out. His first venture which, over time led to the opening of G.I. Joe's, took place in 1946

3

when I was two years old and we were living in Hoquiam, Washington.

Dad got his start in business with a loan from his mother, Mary Orkney. He used the money to bid on down-filled sleeping bags at a government auction at the Fort Lewis army base, located south of Tacoma, Washington. He won the bid and brought the auction lot to Portland. There, Dad placed advertisements in *The Oregonian* and *Oregon Journal* newspapers directing customers to a fruit stand in North Portland that he had rented to use for the sale. The sale was a success with Dad and Mom's brother, Miles Munson, selling out the sleeping bags in three days.

My father continued bidding at government surplus auctions at Fort Lewis and at McChord Air Force Base, also south of Tacoma, and at Pier 91 in Seattle. I understand that veterans were given preference in the auction process which must have been helpful to Dad as a World War II veteran.

He kept selling auction merchandise on street corners and beside roads in the Portland area, and also began selling items wholesale. He would drive from Seattle through Oregon to the California border, selling to war surplus store owners along the way.

Of course, Dad did realize that he could make more money selling from a building compared to selling out of his car. And he wanted to be home with the family instead on the road. It just took a year or so for him to gather the resources to open a store.

In 1947, Dad was able to start selling merchandise in a fixed location. That is when he and Don Metz, another World War II pilot from the Army Air Forces, opened a war surplus store in Salem, Oregon. Mother told me that the partners experimented with the pricing of items. To save making change on transac-

David and I playing in a pup tent in Salem, Oregon, in 1947.

tions, at least some of the items were priced at an even dollar amount. Instead of a price of $3.99 for example, the price would be $4.00.

Many years later, my brother talked to Dad about the rationale behind the even-amount pricing in his first store. Dad related that he had always thought, "Everybody knows the $3.99 is really $4.00. You are not fooling anyone." But, after a while Dad said he began to understand that customers really perceived an item costing $3.99 as much cheaper than one priced at $4.00. That was one of the first basic lessons in retail that Dad learned on the job, and the even-amount pricing strategy was not repeated in later stores.

This Salem war surplus store that Dad was a partner in didn't stay open for long, but it marked a beginning of my family's closer relationship with war surplus merchandise. When Dad was on the road selling auction items to other stores, home and business were somewhat separate. Then, when Dad started his first store, our home and his business came together.

Starting with our Salem home, it seemed like David and I were always surrounded by war surplus or playing and having fun with surplus items. For instance, we would play in a G.I. pup tent in our backyard in Salem, where I could pretend that the tent was a cabin or a fort, or even a castle. As we got older, we would trudge through a nearby vacant lot with small G.I. knapsacks on our backs, imagining we were great explorers, or David would play "army" without me joining in the game.

Sometime in late 1947 or early 1948, we moved to the North Portland area of Kenton to a small, two-bedroom house on Russet Street, which was located a few miles from the Oregon/Washington Interstate Bridge. Many years later, the house would be torn down to make way for an on-ramp to the I-5 Freeway.

But, before that, in the summers of 1948 and 1949, my brother and I enjoyed splashing around in our wading pool in the backyard of the Russet Street house. Do I even have to say wading pool was G.I. surplus? It was a yellow rubber raft which Mom filled with water.

Our inside-out use of the raft proved just how handy war surplus could be. All that was needed was for someone to apply a little creativity to find new uses for items that had been manufactured for use during wartime, and what a bonus if you could have fun doing it! ■

Chapter 2

Six Partners Start 1948 G.I. Joe's

1948 G.I. Joe's. Store's slogan, "Out of Town Shop,"
is partly visible behind parked cars.

I n 1948, Dad and Don Metz, his former Salem store partner, joined with four others in a partnership in another war surplus store venture, according to my mother. The business was located at 8950 N. Vancouver Avenue in North Portland, a few blocks north from where Dad would start up G.I. Joe's as a sole proprietorship four years later. This store was also named G.I. Joe's and the slogan, "out of town shop," was painted on the side of the structure.

Thomas Robinson, of the Historic Photo Archive, discovered an advertisement for G.I. Joe's War Surplus that appeared in *The Oregonian* in February 1948. The ad proclaimed a "store

Part of G.I. Joe's advertisement in the February 26, 1948, Oregonian. Image is top one-third of ad which goes on to list sale items and also claims that there are "Lots of Fine Items for the OUTDOOR OR WORKING MAN."

wide special sale" taking place on Friday and Saturday, February 27 and 28 only.

This advertisement probably ran at the store's opening or shortly after. I believe this because it is the only *Oregonian* display ad I could find for the 1948 G.I. Joe's, and also because the ad told would-be customers to "follow the searchlight." I assume that meant the store was advertising with a bright light shooting up into the night sky, similar to a klieg light used for special events like openings. Incidentally, when my brother read this, he commented that the partners were probably actually using a war surplus search light!

Surplus items mentioned in the ad included large, cotton damask table cloths, one size only, for $1.50 and new spark plugs for 29 cents each. The ad also promoted blue-striped cotton bedspreads for $1.49, two men's t-shirts for $1.35 and "large and thirsty" bath towels for 55 cents.

Shoppers could also pick up a year's supply of silver polish from the Navy for 29 cents and outside white paint, containing lead and zinc, for $2.95 per gallon.

The two really special items mentioned in this G.I. Joe's "out-of-town shop" ad were "sheep-lined, first quality flying pants," for $4.50 and "alpaca-lined flying jackets, Army B-15 Bomber," for $13.95.

I find it interesting that the majority of items advertised, like the table cloths, towels, and paint, are not the kind of items we typically think of today as war surplus items, but of course, they were.

The six-partnered G.I. Joe's was located in the northern outskirts of Portland in a light industrial area. This location made the store stand out from competing army surplus stores, which all seemed to be concentrated in or near downtown Portland.

I discovered this by looking at *Oregonian* newspaper advertisements from 1946 through 1948. I found inexpensive classified ads for war surplus merchandise at Wexport Surplus Sales at N.W. Sixth Avenue and Flanders Street near downtown Portland, and advertisements for sleeping bags at Frank's Army-Navy Store on S.W. Third Avenue near Yamhill Street. Two more downtown stores located on S.W. First Avenue, the Alaska Junk Company and War Surplus Materials, were also advertising war surplus items.

Also, I found *Oregonian* display ads of Pacific Hardware and Electric Company for war surplus merchandise, including sleeping bags, pup tents and tarpaulins. This store was located on S.W. Second Avenue, in downtown Portland, as well.

The only suburban store that I could find advertising war surplus merchandise was Veterans War Surplus Outlet at 126 N.E. Sixteenth Avenue, just off Sandy Boulevard. While this was not a downtown location, it was still centrally sited, only sixteen blocks from the Willamette River and then a short distance over a bridge to downtown.

What I did not find were any ads, either classified or display, for permanent surplus store locations outside of Portland's central area. I don't know whether it was because there were no surplus stores outside of downtown in the late 1940s, or that suburban stores did exist, but just did not advertise.

Whatever the case, this G.I. Joe's, which was the precursor to Dad's sole proprietorship store, was the only suburban surplus store that I know of which ran an *Oregonian* display ad during that time. You could even say that this 1948 G.I. Joe's led the way for stores in selling general merchandise outside of Portland's core, even if the merchandise was war surplus.

The business was housed in former war hospital tents. As you can see from the photo in the next chapter, the store was made up of many of them. The good news about using hospital tents instead of a conventional building was that tents were relatively inexpensive and easy to put up. The bad news was that they did not provide good security against theft. Confirming this, my mother told me that the store was broken into by thieves who slashed through the canvas roof.

Even though the store was located at the edge of Portland when it opened, it did have the advantage of being less than a mile away from Vanport City's 18,700 residents. At the time, Vanport was counted as the second largest city in Oregon and was managed by the Portland Housing Authority.

However, that advantage lasted only until the end of May 1948, when the community was destroyed by a catastrophic flood of the Columbia River. ■

Chapter 3

Portland's 1948 Vanport Flood Leaves Thousands Homeless

Original G.I. Joe's stands above water of Vanport Flood, just north of Portland in late May, 1948. Photo ©Thomas Robinson

Vanport City had been built by Henry Kaiser to provide housing for employees of his Columbia River shipyards during World War II. Most of the housing consisted of two-story, wooden apartment buildings with 14 units, according to the Oregon Historical Society's online

Flood waters float Vanport City apartment buildings just north of Portland, as residents escape on May 30, 1948. Photo ©Thomas Robinson

Floating apartment buildings and debris. 1948 Vanport Flood waters cover first floors of buildings. Photo ©Thomas Robinson

Oregon Encyclopedia, and the community included schools, stores, and even a movie theater.

Vanport was built on the Columbia River floodplain. It was situated at an elevation 15 feet below the top of the dike separating it from Smith Lake to the immediate west, which was fed by the Columbia River. In years of normal spring runoff from the Columbia, the community did not need to be concerned about the possibility of flooding. However, the situation in the spring of 1948 was different, as the Columbia River was running extremely high due to heavier-than-usual snowmelt from the Cascade Mountains. This was because much more snow than normal had fallen during the previous winter, according to what I read in *The Oregonian* from that time.

During the last weekend in May, although the river was running extremely high, officials told Vanport residents that the dikes were sound and that there was no reason to evacuate. That "stay-put and don't worry" message from officials and their representatives continued right up until water broke through a dike on Memorial Day.

It was on Sunday, May 30, at 4:17 p.m., that the unthinkable happened. A 600-foot long break in a dike opened up and a rush of water poured into the Vanport area, rapidly spreading throughout the community!

The water came through a dike break on a railway embankment from Smith Lake to the west, instead of directly from the Columbia, which was north of Vanport. Emergency sirens started sounding in the community but residents had only 35 minutes to evacuate the area, as the water rose so fast.

The flood was devastating. Vanport City was completely inundated, leaving over 18,000 people homeless. Articles in the

May 31, 1948, *Oregonian* describe how the apartment buildings floated off their foundations in the debris-filled water as people scrambled to safety, often with only the belongings they could carry. I read how residents helped each other, including roping children together so they would not be swept away, or helping evacuate children who had been separated from their families.

Some residents lost their cars as well as their homes in the flood, because the traffic jammed up as people tried to drive to higher ground from Vanport.

Surprisingly, only 15 deaths were attributed to the catastrophe. Some have speculated that the death toll was not higher because many residents were elsewhere celebrating Memorial Day and so were not at home to face the water's onslaught.

But whether they had been at home when the water rolled in or not, all Vanport residents were flood victims, and the Red Cross stepped into the chaos to aid them. And it was to the Red Cross that Dad and his partners sold out their store's supply of G.I. sleeping bags, cots and other merchandise to help in the relief effort.

I learned in my research that the 1948 flood occurred in three stages. What I call the first flood stage was the flooding of Vanport City on May 30, and that stage posed the greatest threat to people and housing. After that flooding, the surging water was slowed in its spread east by two other dike systems that ran north and south, but on the afternoon of Monday, May 31, a second dike system failed. A break in a dike of that system allowed the flood water to rush in and cover an area that included the Portland Meadows Racetrack, an outdoor movie theater, and many light industrial businesses. G.I. Joe's at 8950 North Vancouver Avenue was also in this area.

You can see in the aerial photo of G.I. Joe's taken during the flood, that the store was located on higher ground than buildings on the other side of North Vancouver Avenue, like Matheny and Bacon Building Supply. The first floor of that business was inundated and water rose up to its second-floor windows.

However, although G.I. Joe's was on higher ground, looking at the photo, I can see that there must have been some water incursion into the store.

What day did the Red Cross buy the tents, sleeping bags and cots to provide for the flood victims? Was it before this second flood stage? Or was it after, but with the water inside the store so shallow that the merchandise was still OK and undamaged, allowing the Red Cross to buy the relief items? I don't know.

From reading *The Oregonian*, I found that the third flood stage happened about midnight on Monday, May 31. Again, flood water broke through a dike system. This time it raced into the area of small farms and homes to the east of G.I. Joe's, a neighborhood known as Faloma where my family and I would move to, three years later.

Just like in the previously flooded areas, damage was high. Buildings, which in this area were mostly houses and some

G.I. Joe's in center with Matheny and Bacon in lower right, in flood waters during May, 1948 Vanport Flood, just north of Portland, Oregon.
Photo ©Thomas Robinson

barns, floated off their foundations or were covered with water up to their roofs or second stories.

My friend, Lana Blomgren Miller and her family lived in a home on the Columbia River in this third area. Their house was one of about ten built on the dike, so these river-side houses were at a higher elevation than nearby neighbors.

Lana gave this eye-witness account of the flood. She wrote that she remembers looking out of her house and only being able to "see the tops of the roofs of the houses across the street," and then going into her house and looking down the stairs to see the party room covered with four feet of water.

Lana continued, "You might remember that we had a white stucco house. My Dad could never cover up the water line across the back from the flood." Another memory she shared was getting a first-hand view of the flood's devastation when the dad of her friend, Nancy Sells, took her and Nancy out on the river "in his amphibious duck," and they saw "houses from Vanport floating around."

Lana wrote, "We were so lucky living on the dike." As the river lowered after the flood, she said, "Dad cleaned up our silt-filled backyard with fire hoses; the water was pumped from the Columbia." Lana concluded, "I was only five years old, but the emotion and feeling of fear from my parents is still alive."

When the flood waters receded throughout the floodplain, the second and third flooded areas eventually returned to their previous uses, but the Vanport area did not. The housing was not rebuilt and the thousands of people who had lived there had to find other places to live.

In its place today is the Portland International Raceway, or PIR as it is known, and a golf course. Also, the I-5 Freeway now runs through the Columbia floodplain where Vanport used to be and to the west of where the 1948 and 1952 G.I. Joe's stores were located.

After the 1948 Vanport Flood, there were two more flood threats. There was a huge flood scare in the spring of 1956, prior to The Dalles Dam becoming operational, and a smaller flood worry around Christmas Day in 1964. Both times, the Columbia River ran high, but did not break through protective dikes.

While the land in that floodplain is still at the same low elevation today as it was in 1948, the Columbia River has since been controlled by so many dams that it no longer has the power to threaten severe flooding in a late spring because of heavy snowmelt. Never again will a majority of residents living near the Columbia north of Portland have to worry about losing their lives, homes and belongings to the raging river. ■

Chapter 4

The Partners' G.I. Joe's Continues & Dad Opens War Surplus Liquidators

Surplus Liquidators owned by Dad and partner in 1950 in Southeast Portland.

The G.I. Joe's in North Portland remained in business after the 1948 flood of late May and early June. Evidently the partners also owned a second G.I. Joe's in a southeast Portland suburb, located on 82nd Avenue between Division and Powell Streets, which continued in business, as well. I do not remember hearing of that store as a kid, but Thomas Robinson of the Historic Photo Archive found listings and addresses for the two stores in Portland's 1948 phone book.

Both stores were also listed in the 1950 Portland phone book, but the address of the North Portland store changed from 8950 to 8700 N. Vancouver. That was the location Dad would take over in two years.

Then, in the 1951 Portland phone book, only the G.I. Joe's

Closeup of Dad standing in doorway of Surplus Liquidators in 1950.

on North Vancouver Avenue appeared, so the one on S.E. 82nd Avenue must have closed before the directory was published.

However, Dad's partnership in the early G.I. Joe's must have concluded by October, 1949, or sooner. That is because, a one-paragraph news brief in *The Oregonian* on October 8 of that year, described him as the store manager of War Surplus Liquidators in southeast Portland. The paragraph reported the robbery of two B-15 flying jackets and a pair of boots from the store.

I was aware of War Surplus Liquidators as a kid, but thought that the store opened in 1951. I also thought that Dad was the only owner, but Thomas Robinson gave me different information on both start date and ownership. Tom told me the 1950 Portland City Directory listed Dad as a partner in the business with G. G. Schuyler. So, the store was in operation in 1950, and, the date of the robbery report in *The Oregonian* shows that the business was started by the fall of 1949, if not sooner.

The War Surplus Liquidators store was located on S.E. 82nd Avenue, near Foster Road. Like G.I. Joe's, it was housed in a hospital tent with wooden walls on the exterior. I was five years old in 1949 and this is the first of Dad's stores I can vaguely remember. The entrance had three or four wooden steps and the business name was written in large letters across the front of the store's wooden face. The hospital tent peaked many times along the roofline.

Over the door was a sign with Dad's slogan, which he continued to use with G.I. Joe's. "Come in and browse around," it said, welcoming shoppers.

Mom poses Easter morning in 1951 in Pasadena at my maternal grandparents' home.

This store did not last long. Even though the 1951 Portland City Directory still listed War Surplus Liquidators as owned by Dad and G. G. Schuyler, I think that Dad had left that partnership by the spring of 1951.

I know it was that spring that my parents decided to check out Los Angeles as a possible place for Dad to start yet another business.

My family headed to Southern California and we stayed with

Mom's parents in Pasadena, but not for long. Dad was a son of the Pacific Northwest through and through, and my family soon headed back to Portland.

Dad's next business venture was the one he finally settled on, to build and grow for the rest of his life. Five or six years after he started selling surplus out of his car or beside roads, he finally got it right.

The business opportunity happened, either later in 1951 or early in 1952, when Dad heard that the G.I. Joe's store at 8700 North Vancouver Avenue in Portland was for sale. He bought the business on his own this time, unlike the three prior stores which he had owned with partners.

Dad did keep the G.I. Joe's name, but the new store was now his to run and stock as he wished, and he was ready to go. And who can say? Perhaps it took Dad's five or six years of experience with different ways of selling in different locations with different business associates, for him to be prepared to make the most of this opportunity to start a store on his own. But whatever the reason, at this point Dad had the skills, motivation and resources to build this business.

And although there may be a lot that we don't know now about how Dad started that small store in a hospital tent in North Portland, we do know it was the beginning of a business that grew for almost 60 years, and, some would even say, became a Pacific Northwest icon in the process. ■

Chapter 5

Growing G.I. Joe's

*Early G.I. Joe's before change from tent structure
to wooden one, circa 1952.*

The 1952 G.I. Joe's owned by Dad was still in a hospital tent like the 1948 store was. It was a very basic structure for a store. And the parking lot was basic, too. Instead of a layer of gravel or blacktop, the ground was covered with roofing tabs. These narrow asphalt shingles clumped together to form a barrier against mud when it rained.

Behind the store was the Columbia Slough, which was a deep ditch about 50 feet wide filled with slow-moving water. Fishermen would come to stand along its banks and fish for carp and catfish there.

Although the 18,000 residents of Vanport City did not live nearby anymore, G.I. Joe's was still situated well for a retail business. Back in those days prior to the I-5 Freeway, the store was located to take advantage of traffic on nearby Union Avenue (now Martin Luther King, Jr. Boulevard) going to and from the Interstate Bridge between Portland and Vancouver, Washington.

G.I. Joe's was the first store of its kind located on the Oregon side of the bridge.

I believe this unique location, a few miles away from Vancouver, was one of the major reasons for Dad's initial success. Because Washington had sales tax and Oregon did not, the store had great appeal to Vancouver residents.

The merchandise included a variety of army/navy surplus, which was also a draw. There was a lack of consumer goods after the war and quite a demand for government issued items that could be used for outdoor recreation. Sleeping bags, cots, tents, and canteens were not being manufactured in quantities for domestic use yet, so everyone bought them as G.I. surplus. This merchandise really pulled people in the door.

Cheap cigarettes were a draw, too. Customers wouldn't buy them by the packs but by the carton, and often would buy many cartons at a time. To make them easy to carry, employees at the front counter would tie the cartons together with string from an overhead dispenser.

Again, there was a special incentive for shoppers from Washington to buy their cigarettes from G.I. Joe's. Not only would they not have to pay sales tax, they also would not have to pay the cigarette tax that was levied by the State of Washington, according to my brother.

It is easy to be judgmental about smoking cigarettes today, but it was not until 1964 that the U.S. Surgeon General presented the ground-breaking report on the health risks of smoking. And it took another year for health warnings to be required on cigarette packs. Prior to the 1964 report, smoking cigarettes was widely thought to be relaxing, with no ill effects.

Dad soon started upgrading G.I. Joe's. First, he replaced the

1956 addition to G.I. Joe's doubled the store's size.

hospital tent with a small wooden building. The lack of security for the merchandise when the store was based in a tent must have fueled Dad's desire to upgrade quickly.

David recently reminded me that prior to the tent replacement, Dad and his general manager, Art Bruer, along with others, took turns sleeping in the tent-store at night in order to prevent robberies. David said that a German shepherd dog also stayed with the person on watch duty for added security.

In 1956, the first addition to the small wood building was constructed. It doubled the store's size. At this time, the G.I. Joe's sign was mounted over the entrance, visible to drivers coming from both the north and south. There was a sign advertising the price of a carton of cigarettes that jutted out over the parking lot, and other signs advertising merchandise were posted on the front of the building, as well.

Then, in 1960, the first concrete tilt-up expansion was added, doubling the store's footage again.

What I remember about the inside of the store in the early years, were aisles of wooden bins, filled with G.I. surplus treasures. One bin was filled with small bottles of insect repellent, resembling large bottles of vanilla extract. One Saturday morning when I was around nine years old, I went to work with Dad.

He told me to "neaten" the insect repellent bin. First, I wiped off the bottles with a cloth. Next, I gathered up the bottles that were lying haphazardly on top of each other and stood them up, pushing them into one corner of the bin. I thought I had done such a good job of cleaning and organizing!

Then, my father came by and gave me my first lesson in retailing. He told me to make sure the bottles were clean, but to mess them up again, so that it looked like there was more merchandise and like customers had been going through the bin.

I discovered that cleaning in the store was definitely not like helping Mom clean our house! ■

Chapter 6

Surrounded by Surplus, Even at Home

My family celebrating our first Christmas in home on Columbia Avenue, north of Portland in 1951.

M y family moved to a house on a half-acre lot in Multnomah County north of Portland in the summer of 1951. The street we lived on was Columbia Avenue, which has since been renamed and is now an extension of N.E. Gertz Road. The area where we lived was a mix of small farms, a mobile home park, a small housing tract, and houses on an acre or so of land. And G.I. Joe's was just a mile away, on North Vancouver Avenue.

The house was built on the floodplain of the Columbia River, which was about a half mile north of us. While the original store had not been inundated in the 1948 flood, this house had been. In 1951, when we moved in, there was still dried mud from the flood waters on the floor of an unfinished room on the second floor!

Our house was a medium-sized, two-story traditional, with an unfinished basement, where inventory for the store was kept. There, next to Mom's clothes washer and a

Army surplus and ballet lessons seemed like a normal mix to me.

ping-pong table, were piles of army knapsacks, canteens with holders and belts, stacks of inflatable rubber rafts, empty ammunition boxes, and other surplus items.

It did not seem unusual to me. That was just the way our basement was, serving as the first warehouse for the store. And the smell from the basement was just the way it was, too. If you opened the door in the garage to the descending wooden stairs, the fragrance of army surplus would waft up from the basement and surround you.

The sight and smell of army surplus were not unusual for David and his friends, either, when they came to Cub Scout meetings in our basement. Mom was Den Leader for a while

David holds our new puppy, Tarps in 1951.

and I remember the boys gathered around the ping pong table surrounded by surplus, while painting bear heads made out of plaster of Paris.

Not only did G.I. Joe's take up space in our home, it also took up space in family conversations. As we sat down for dinner together, our conversation would include not only what each of us had done during the day, but also what the store's sales had been for the day or week. Dad enjoyed sharing information with us and liked to tell us what was selling well.

During one dinner, we heard that there had been a huge sale of tarpaulins, which are waterproof, canvas covers to keep things dry or rig up as a tent. We celebrated that sale by naming our new cocker spaniel puppy, Tarps or Tarpsy. She was a sweet dog, named in honor of a sweet sale.

The whole family worked for the store. When I was about nine years old, I began going to work with Dad on occasional Saturday mornings. Besides "neatening the bins," I would straighten shoes, matching up misplaced pairs, and then dust them. My brother, David, who was then around seven years old, would sweep floors or sort fish hooks. When he got older, he was given the more challenging job of cleaning off the rust-preventa-

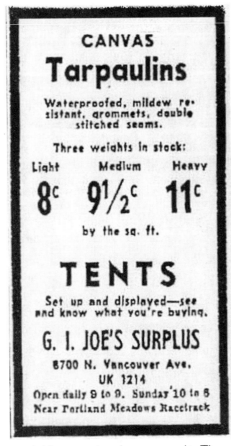

Ad for tarpaulins that appeared in The Oregonian, *March 21, 1952. Was it a similar ad in 1951 that led to the big sale we celebrated by getting a puppy?*

tive, Cosmoline, from small army surplus tools. This was done by soaking the items in diesel fuel and then wiping them off. Mom, who had a background in bookkeeping, contributed by preparing the payroll checks.

David and I even worked at home. G.I. Joe's carried hardware as well as surplus. Sitting on the hearth in the evening, our job was to screw nuts on bolts, so that a set would be easier to buy. Customers would not have to search through separate bins for nuts and bolts to find matches.

We got paid a penny for each 10 units, or 10 cents for 100 nuts and bolts. This was Dad's way of teaching us that, to make money, you had to work. As we were working he would tell us, "Money is stored-up working hours." David remembers making $1.80 one day, which was one heck of a lot of nuts and bolts to screw together!

The most exciting job that David and I had at the store was

selling fireworks in the parking lot, in a little booth. I think that was in 1956. I felt very grownup, even though we only sold sparklers, snakes and smoke. However, I guess Dad did not consider David and me completely grownup, because I later heard that we were being checked on frequently by employees to make sure that we were OK.

Now and then, David and I would get to go along with Dad on his trip to the wholesaler, Bernstein Brothers in downtown Portland, to pick up cases of cigarettes and candy. The store sold a lot of cigarettes, and I'll bet that Dad was smoking his brand, Lucky Strikes, as we drove there in his red Chevy pickup truck. However, my brother and I would not be thinking about that. We would be focused on the candy bars we would be sure to receive.

David remembers that Jules, who was always smoking a cigar, was our favorite Bernstein brother. Jules was the one who would always surreptitiously slip a candy bar to my brother and me, pretending that the gift was a secret from our dad. Of course Dad knew and had given his permission, but the whole charade made the candy taste that much better to us!

Incidentally, Dad smoked cigarettes pretty much non-stop while I was growing up, and I have to give kudos to him for quitting smoking permanently in 1956. However, it just might have been easier for him to stop his smoking habit than it is for me to change my memories of him! Whenever I remember my childhood, I always picture Dad smoking. ■

*Dad smoked his omnipresent cigarette
as I received my first bike from Grandpa.*

Chapter 7

Dad Flies Bombers in World War II

My parents, Charmian and Edward Orkney took time to visit the Alamo in San Antonio, Texas, in September 1942, during Dad's flight training.

avid and I knew that our dad had been a B-24 bomber pilot in World War II and that he had served in the South Pacific in New Guinea. We were aware that he had the rank of Captain when he left the service. We also knew that he was in the Jolly Rogers Heavy Bomb Group, and that the symbol for the Jolly Rogers on the tail of his plane had

Jolly Rogers logo that appeared on tail of B-24 Dad flew.

looked like a pirate flag. But instead of displaying a skull and crossed bones, it showed a skull with two crossed bombs under it.

Another fact I was aware of was that my dad was serving overseas when I was born in 1944. The story was that he and his crew received a bottle of whiskey in celebration of my birth, and their latrine ended up getting burned down in the celebration!

That was about all my brother and I knew of Dad's time in the Army Air Forces when we were kids, because Dad did not talk to us about it, staying quiet about his service in World War II as so many of his fellow veterans did. It was not until a few years ago that an older cousin of mine, Bruce Orkney of Seattle, told me more.

Bruce told me that with all the combat missions Dad flew, "He and his crew returned unscathed every time. That was remarkable; he was very proud of that!" Bruce continued, "He was the squadron leader and later the group leader, always the number one plane on their bombing runs."

Bruce thought that Dad flew 52 bombing runs, but it was actually 58 runs according to a story in a 1944 newspaper clipping I received from my cousin, Mary Orkney Conlon, after I had talked with her brother Bruce about Dad's time in the service.

The clipping did not include the name of the newspaper or reporter, although the short article said dad was interviewed by a

*Ed Orkney, bomber pilot in New Guinea, poses for a photo.
Note the wool-lined boots. Photo taken in 1943 or 1944.*

"Washingtonian." It must have been dated around August 26, 1944, because that was the date on another byline in the clipping.

The interview that ended up in the short article in the unknown newspaper took place in Seattle when Dad was on his way home to Hoquiam from his overseas tour of duty. It said Dad spent 11 months in the South Pacific and that his service consisted of 58 missions and 386 combat hours, and, that after a furlough of several weeks, my dad would be reporting for reassignment.

Also in the article, Dad gave the opinion that the war was "going pretty well from our point of view."

Looking back to the beginning of Dad's service in the armed forces, he enlisted in the Army Reserves in September, 1940. After the Japanese bombed Pearl Harbor in December 1941, he was moved out of the Reserves and into an Army Artillery Unit and from there transferred into the Army Air Corps, which was the branch of the Army Air Forces that trained recruits.

He took flight training in Texas and graduated from flight school in Altus, Oklahoma, in April 1943. Sometime after that, in the late summer or early fall, he shipped out to serve in the Fifth Army Air Force in the Southwest Pacific Theater on the island of New Guinea.

He was assigned to the 90th Bomb Group, known as the Jolly Rogers, with the slogan, "the best damn heavy bomb group in the world."

The only details of his time there flying a B-24 Liberator bomber came from another clipping my cousin Mary Lynne sent me, which I assume was from the local Hoquiam newspaper. The short article had a byline of May 29 (1944), from the "Advance Echelon, Fifth Air Force, Somewhere in New Guinea," and said that Dad took part in the "first mass-daylight raid on Hollandia," a Japanese airbase and stronghold in Dutch New Guinea.

The article went on to say that Hollandia had "recently been invaded by American troops in a seaborne assault that carried the base," and that "fighting was still in progress."

That is it. That is the only information I have of any of Dad's bombing runs when he was serving in the 90th Bomb Group, and I am grateful to my cousin for sending the two news clippings from that time.

My brother was able to find out more as an adult and talking to my dad. What stood out for him was Dad telling him that the Jolly Rogers suffered losses of about 40%, mainly due to adverse weather conditions. But when you consider that the pilots flew those heavily-laden planes across the empty Pacific to

Edward Orkney In Hollandia Raid

ADVANCE ECHELON, FIFTH AIR FORCE, SOMEWHERE IN NEW GUINEA, May 29.—(Special.)—Pilot of a Liberator bomber in the famous 'Jolly Roger' bomb unit, First Lieutenant Edward M. Orkney, of Hoquiam, Washington, was one of the airmen who flew on the first mass daylight raid on Hollandia, Jap airbase and stronghold in Dutch New Guinea. Hollandia was recently invaded by American troops in a seaborne assault that carried the base. Fighting is still in progress.

Former University of Washington student, Lieutenant Orkney is the son of Mr. and Mrs. R. W. Orkney, 712 First street Hoquiam. His wife and two-months-old daughter, Jenna Lee, live in Hoquiam.

Lieutenant Orkney won his wings in April, 1943, after previously having served as a technical sergeant in the Coast Artillery.

Yellowed newspaper clipping about bombing run to Hollandia in May 1944 that Dad flew in.

a small island or group of islands, it is amazing to me that the losses of men and planes were not higher.

The B-24 crews were flying without what we take for granted today. They had no radar, no computers to figure out where they were going. Instead, navigators on board computed the route. Plus, the planes carried only as much fuel as needed in order to reach their target and then return to their base. I ask myself now, "How did they do it?"

And we have to remember that even taking off with a load of bombs was risky. I once mentioned to Dad as an adult that I didn't like landing when I was flying somewhere. He was amused and commented that landings were the easy part when he was flying bombers. He said that the challenge was getting the bombers airborne on take-off when they were heavy with bombs.

But as I said, I did not know any of this when I was a kid. My dad was just my dad, and the visible link to his time as a bomber pilot was that he always wore khaki shirts and pants like he did in the service.

One memory I have of my dad, dressed in khakis of course, is of him holding a G.I. flamethrower, with the wand in one hand and the tank in the other. He was standing in what we called our Back 40, which was a large grassy field behind our house. Dad was shooting flames on the vegetation as a way of clearing the field. The grass and weeds did indeed burn up, and thankfully, the house did not.

Dad also attempted to come to the rescue of the driver of the view-impaired school bus that David and I sometimes rode to school. In the frequently rainy winter, it could get quite steamy inside the bus, and David and I noticed that our driver was having a hard time keeping the windshield clear so that he could see. We told Dad about the problem, and he brought home a small, boxy device for us to give to our bus driver. I believe it was a portable G.I. defroster.

However, when our driver placed it on the bus dashboard and gave it a try, it had no noticeable effect on the condensation on the windshield. It was too bad the defroster didn't work as well as the flamethrower. ■

Chapter 8

Hunting for Army Surplus Treasures

1956 sign at G.I. Joe's entrance advertising a carton of cigarettes for $1.70.

In the 1950s, G.I. Joe's was an especially fun place to visit. On a trip to the store, customers never knew what they would discover in the bins full of merchandise. Canteens, plastic army helmet liners, ammunition belts, knapsacks, insect repellent, even the reflecting part of a tank periscope—these were just some of the items they might find. What would buyers do with these items? That was limited only by their creativity and imagination.

The store's bins were not only treasure troves for adults, but for children, too. Years after the original surplus store was gone, folks would tell me about shopping there when they were kids, usually going to the store along with their fathers. They would reminisce about what a treat it had been to come to G.I. Joe's and would often tell me details of special items they had found.

I heard so many stories about customers' experiences in the old store that I came to realize that it was not just a place to shop, but also a place to be entertained. As customers roamed the aisles, they could check out the latest merchandise and ponder how to put it to good use. That use could be for play, like boys using knapsacks from G.I. Joe's in army games, or an item could be used in a practical way, like adults sprinkling G.I. foot powder, bought at the store, in their socks before they went hiking.

The war surplus merchandise also offered a preview of coming commercial outdoor recreational gear for customers. That is because so much of the government-issued surplus that was sold at the store was not yet being manufactured on a large scale for the civilian market.

The merchandise which had been made for use by our armed forces fighting in World War II could now be sold at home for peaceful use. The army sleeping bags, cots, tents, tarps, canteens, mess kits, and other equipment that Dad bought at auction could now be enjoyed by G.I. Joe's customers in the great outdoors. And sometimes an item could be used in an unusual way, like making a wading pool for kids to splash in out of a G.I. life raft.

Also, the store sold more than army/navy surplus, and this made it different from many similar stores. G.I. Joe's always carried cigarettes in that era, and shoes and work boots, tools, and heavy hardware were in the product mix, too. The variety of products made it very hard to categorize the business.

Some of the merchandise, like cigarettes, drew customers from a wide area, while merchandise like heavy hardware and tools mainly attracted nearby business people. But, however far from the store customers lived or worked, they were drawn to the store by its unusual product mix. ■

Growing up with G.I. Joe's

Chapter 9

A Unique Neighborhood to Explore and Enjoy

Our home on Columbia Avenue in a rural area north of Portland in 1951.

I n many ways, the area where we lived in those early years was a lot like G.I. Joe's. The neighborhood was hard to categorize, but full of treasures if you were open to finding them. For instance, there was farmland that provided entertainment to the rear of our house and between our house and the store. The land was planted in cucumbers that were crop-dusted by small airplanes. I loved watching the planes fly low and then pull up sharply at the end of rows. It was almost like watching an air show.

Then, when the cucumbers were ripe, they were picked by inmates from the county jail. My imagination would fire up, as I wondered what would happen if a prisoner escaped during cucumber picking.

Across the street from our house was more peaceful entertainment. A dairy cow grazed there, in a field which was part of a small family farm. David and I got to be friends with Randy and his sister, who lived there with their grandparents for a while. We would go over to the hay-filled barn some late afternoons at milking time, and their grandfather was kind enough to let us try milking. These neighbors also raised chickens, and we would go to their house to buy eggs.

Randy was full of mischief. In my fourth-grade class, he told a substitute teacher that I had called her a witch on the school bus the day before. It was true, and I can't recall if I was punished for it, but I surely was upset with Randy!

Next door was a kennel where we got our puppy, Tarps. It was named the Flo-Bob Kennel, for owners Florence and Bob who raised cocker spaniels.

I am sure there was a variety of wildlife on the land, but what I remember are the pheasants, red-winged blackbirds, and caterpillars. The adult male pheasants were multi-colored and beautiful, as they flew across the sky or searched for food in our Back 40. One afternoon, I looked out our kitchen window to see that our neighbor's weeping willow tree was covered with pheasants perched on its branches. I was enthralled! It looked like a scene on a blue and white plate from China.

David and I once took part in a baby pheasant rescue attempt with neighbor kids Fred Rau and his sister, Karen Krafsic. I think it was Fred and Karen's mother who found some abandoned pheasant hatchlings and tried to keep them warm on a tray in their oven, which was set at a very low temperature. I remember peering over the oven door along with Fred, Karen, and David to check on the tiny birds. They did not survive, despite our efforts. I think they were just too young.

*A Girl Scout, a Cub Scout and a trusty dog
sit in front of the Christmas tree in 1954.*

The red-winged blackbirds, with their distinctive call, could be seen and heard as they clung to cattail stalks in the slough that David and I passed by on our walks to Columbia School. I loved to see the flash of crimson on their wings as they flew by.

As for the fuzzy caterpillars, so soft to the touch, they formed a colony in our backyard birch tree. However, their colony proved no match for the G.I. flame thrower that my dad wielded.

There were many wonderful things about living in this Columbia River area, but I did not like the small sloughs which ran on one side of the road leading to our school. The sloughs were on both sides of the road on the way to G.I. Joe's and the small grocery store at the mobile home park where David and I sometimes liked to shop. These sloughs were three or four feet wide, filled with turgid, brown water. I was always concerned about the possibility of falling in, especially if I was riding my bike.

Adding to the area's eclectic mix were the Columbia Edgewater Golf Course and the Portland Yacht Club, both of which we passed on our way to and from school.

Some of my schoolmates lived in homes along the Columbia, with their backyards sloping down to the water. Many of these homes had been partially flooded in 1948, just like our home three years before we moved in. There was also an anchorage with a network of docks below the yacht club that I enjoyed visiting with my friend, Nancy Sells, whose father had a boat repair business there.

But one place I did not go was to Tomahawk Island in the middle of the river channel between Oregon and Washington. When I looked across the Columbia River, while standing firmly on the dike above my school, the island looked like a magical place to me. It was sandy and flat, covered with small trees and bushes. I was sure that if only I could go there, it would be so special. I even imagined that I might find buried treasure on the island.

I finally got to explore the island as a teenager, when Dad got a ski boat that my family took out on weekends for a few summers. We would go boating and water skiing on the Columbia, ever on the lookout for submerged logs. On one boating excursion, we stopped at Tomahawk Island, and I found that it wasn't magical, nor did I find any buried treasure. So I just had to be content with the picnic treasure of Mom's fried chicken, which, incidentally, was really good.

Portland Meadows Horse Racing Track was near our home, to the west of G.I. Joe's. At Columbia School, children of people who worked with the horses would attend for the part of the

*David walking up the beach at Rooster Rock State Park
in the Columbia River Gorge in 1960. My family would go there
to swim and sunbathe in the summer.*

year that racing was taking place. Their parents were also frequent customers of G.I. Joe's.

My family would attend the races now and then at Portland Meadows, and I loved the pageantry of sound and sight. Each race began with a dramatic bugle call as the jockeys rode their horses out on the race track, cantering by spectators in the grandstand. That was when I would delight in the many color combinations of the jockeys' racing silks. Then the horses and jockeys would get in place at the starting gate. Next, a bell would sound and the announcer would intone, "And there they go," as the horses dashed out of the gate and streamed down the track.

After the horses and jockeys crossed the finish line, the race pageantry would be capped by the winning horse and rider parading by the grandstand to the winner's circle. There, they would be met by the horse's owner and trainer. I even got to take part in one winner's ceremony as a teenager when I presented a blanket to the owner of the victorious horse on Valentine's Day, which was also my birthday. My parents had funded the blanket as a special gift to me, so that I could make the presentation then, wearing my red top and white skirt with red hearts on it. I wouldn't be surprised if I had worn white gloves, too!

Obviously, the neighborhood where I grew up was quite different from most urban neighborhoods of the 1950s. Not far from where we lived were farmers, places with horses, a golf club, a yacht club, and a horse racing track. Slightly further away was the Portland Airport; cookie and cracker maker, Nabisco; and a meat-packing plant.

To the north was Hayden Island. That was where the amusement park, Jantzen Beach, was located, with its gigantic roller coaster and huge swimming pools. Every June for two or three years, David and I took swimming lessons in the shallow pool next to the deep one with the incredibly tall high dive. Let's just say that at lesson time, the sky always seemed to be gray and cloudy, while temperatures hovered in the 60s and we shivered in the pool.

Also on Hayden Island was one of my favorite places, the Columbia Riding Academy, where I took English riding lessons for a short time. I so wanted to have a horse of my own to keep in our Back 40 and thought that my parents would let me get one if I became a proficient rider. Well, I did not become an equestrian, and I did not get a horse! I had to be content with filling a sketch pad with drawings of horses.

On Hayden Island, too, was Waddles Restaurant. At Waddles, we kids got a paper bib with a picture of a waddling duck on it, and we got to ride a small metal horse in the waiting area before being seated for dinner.

We also lived close to Vancouver, Washington, with our home

just a few miles from the Interstate Bridge that crossed the Columbia River. When Dad would take one of his regular trips to the Tacoma area to buy more G.I. surplus, Mom would often take David and me to The Holland Restaurant in Vancouver for a dinner of crisp, buttery waffles. My brother and I felt like we were getting away with something, because we didn't have to eat any vegetables on those nights.

Where we lived was unique. We had a great variety of locales, homes, businesses, and things to do, close to our home. I like to think that the area was like a mirror to G.I. Joe's. The store and our neighborhood offered such a variety of opportunities for exploration and creativity. And there was nothing fancy or pretentious about Dad's store or the neighborhood we lived in. Both were just "down home." ■

Growing up with G.I. Joe's

Chapter 10

Singing the Song of the Columbia

Photo from 1958 Yearbook of Columbia School in Multnomah County, north of Portland, Oregon, courtesy of Fred Rau

The Columbia River dominated the area where my family and I lived, and many of the important places nearby were named after it. This included Columbia Avenue, where our home was, and Columbia School, where David and I went to elementary school.

We lived about one-half mile from the Columbia River, from 1951 through 1956, and there was a downside to living so close to this force of nature, because the river was still untamed then and our home was on the river's floodplain.

Even though Bonneville Dam and the mighty Grand Coulee Dam straddled the Columbia, these dams and others on the river had not stopped the damaging 1948 flood in our area. It took The Dalles Dam, which went into operation in 1957, to put an end to the risk of severe local flooding.

In the meantime, my family and other residents of the floodplain paid a lot of attention to the Columbia, especially during the first season of the year. That was the time of melting snow in the Cascade Mountains, which created the spring runoff, making the Columbia run fast and high, swelled with new volume.

So, in the spring, residents wanted to know: What was the depth of the snowpack in the mountains? How fast was the snow melting into the Columbia's tributaries in Canada and on into Washington, Idaho and Oregon? How high was the river, and how fast was it rising? Were the temperatures in the Cascades higher than usual, which would lead to a more rapid melt and higher spring runoff? And at what height did local experts predict that the Columbia would crest in our area?

Before that, in the late fall and winter, we would start keeping tabs on snow in the Cascades. Did the snow start falling in November or December? Once snowfall began, how frequent were the snow storms?

Obviously, we paid attention to the Columbia River and its tributaries because it could personally affect us. The 1948 Vanport Flood was too fresh in everyone's minds, with so many of our neighbors having lived through it. Those memories prompted the unspoken question in our minds every spring: Will the river flood this year?

But instead of voicing this worry, we focused on things that could be measured, like spring temperatures in the mountains, the height of the Columbia in relation to the protective dikes that ringed our area, or reports from engineers on the strength of these dikes.

It could be stressful living so close to the river, but there was also an upside for me. I am sure that I became more attuned to nature than if I had lived in a typical suburb. It became automatic for me to check the river when close by, looking at water color, height, and flow. I didn't check it consciously or for any particular reason, unless it was during spring runoff time. Rather, the river was an important part of my environment and so I paid attention to it.

And while paying attention to the river as a kid, I grew to love it. The Columbia's power and majesty in those days, as it rolled to the sea, is something that is still deep in my heart.

In fact, I now find it somewhat hard to drive up the Columbia River Gorge and look at the placid river, which is just a pale suggestion of what it used to be before all the hydroelectric dams slowed it down. I know the Columbia's potential is to run fast and free, filled gloriously with swimming salmon. That is what I see in my mind's eye, in contrast to the present-day, smooth river that I can see out my car window driving in the Gorge on I-84.

I remember a special spring day in 1956, when Mom and Dad took David and me up the Columbia Gorge in order to see Native Americans fishing the traditional way at Celilo Falls. I didn't know what to expect.

Then I found myself in awe, as I watched the fishermen with their nets and spears, leaning out to catch salmon from flimsy and wet wooden platforms, above the crashing, roiling water!

*David, Dad and I view Celilo Falls
in the Columbia River Gorge,
Oregon, in 1956.*

How could the men fish that way, when a slip off a platform could mean sudden death?

What my family and I observed was part of the last spring salmon run through Celilo Falls before the fishing site was destroyed in March 1957. That is when The Dalles Dam backed up the Columbia River and inundated the falls.

All of us who live or have lived in the Pacific Northwest lost an incredible legacy when Celilo Falls was covered with water. I wish I had understood then, the huge significance of what we were seeing at the fishing site that spring, but how could I have? I don't think that even today we give it the significance it deserves!

Native Americans fishing for the last spring in 1956 at Celilo Falls, Columbia Gorge, Oregon. Photo by Charmian Orkney

What I do know is that I am so grateful to my parents for giving David and me the gift of seeing the Native Americans fishing in the traditional way at Celilo Falls during the last spring, ever, that the salmon would challenge the falls as fishermen tried to gather them up.

And it is obvious that the fishing was a crucial part of the celebration of spring, renewal and community by the Tribal People that had taken place every year for centuries at this site, also known as Wy-am.

It amazes me today that I got to be there! I got to take part in that celebration, too! It was in a very small way, but I was at

Celilo that spring day as a 12-year-old witness from down-river, wearing my special pink dress for the occasion, with my mom and dad and brother.

I think back to the roar of Celilo Falls that I heard then. To me, now, it is a hymn to the Creator, celebrated by the Umatilla, Yakima, Warm Springs, Nez Perce and other tribes as well. Members of these tribes are the Native Americans who fished, traded and celebrated life on, and beside, the majestic Columbia for generations beyond count, for 10,000 years or more.

And while we no longer can hear that magnificent reverberation of falling water with our ears, it still exists in collective memory, if we will but listen.

And I believe that those of us who hold the Columbia River in our hearts, no matter who we are or where we live, still share in that song of praise that was raised up to our Creator by the roaring water of Celilo Falls. ■

Chapter 11

Flood Threat Close to Home

I n late spring of 1956, there was a serious flood scare for those of us living on the Columbia River floodplain north of Portland. Dad was so worried about the threat that he attached our house to its foundation, placing heavy cable over the roof and looping it through metal hooks that he installed on the front and back of the cement base.

Dad knew of the damage and loss created by the Vanport Flood eight years before, and he wanted to make sure that our house didn't float off its foundation in another flood.

That spring, the Columbia River was again running very high, and residents of the floodplain were feeling threatened. Of course, there were far fewer residents worrying about a possible flood in 1956 compared to 1948. That was because of the thousands of Vanport residents who had been forced to relocate when their housing was destroyed in the 1948 flood. They never returned to the area because Vanport had not been rebuilt.

In 1948, I had been too young to be concerned about rising waters, but this time I was well aware of the situation. The threat of a flood became personal for me because the people worrying about it included my family and friends.

And the possibility of another catastrophic flood happening in 1956 was real. Some of my friends from school who lived on the Columbia saw their backyards disappear beneath the rising river. Kathy McCuddy Johnson's family lived on the river, and she told me the water rose so high in the backyards of water-front homes, that she and neighboring classmates rowed boats from one yard to another to visit each other.

That sounds like fun, but the damage caused by the encroaching water was not. Kathy says, "The water came into our daylight basement, which opened onto the backyard facing the river. Sandbags were placed five feet high across the patio to keep the flooding at a minimum. But even then, there was water seepage and thus damage to our home's interior on the lower floor. There was an attempt to raise some furniture, including our piano, up onto wooden blocks, which saved some pieces."

Lana Blomgren Miller, whose family also lived on the Columbia, agreed with Kathy, saying the high water was "fun for us kids because we paddled around our backyards in rubber rafts…"

Although residents with waterfront homes on the Columbia River were experiencing some flooding at that point, the rest of us on the floodplain were not. But the possibility was there; the river had not yet crested, and we weren't sure how high it would rise. But we did know that if the river broke through a dike, water would come rolling in to cover the area where we lived.

My parents were very concerned and eventually decided it would be best if only Dad stayed in the house while the Columbia was in the late runoff stage that spring. Mom, David, and I would go elsewhere. We could have stayed in the Portland area, but Mom had a different idea.

Leaving Dad to face the possibility of flood, Mom drove David and me to Disneyland! The park was almost brand new, having been open for just a year.

After worrying about dirty, debris-filled water surging into

*David and I visit the Mission San Juan Capistrano
during Southern California trip in 1956.*

our house, I know I was both relieved and delighted to be at the "magic kingdom." What a contrast for me, as well as Mom and David! But it felt a little unreal to me to be basking in the Southern California sunshine when we knew what Dad and our friends were possibly facing. However, I was still determined to enjoy Disneyland. I know that I did, but all I remember clearly is speeding a miniature car around on a miniature freeway.

Mom also took us to the San Juan Capistrano Mission in Orange County, where legend says that swallows return from their winter home on a certain day in March every year. David and I found plenty of birds, but the photo shows it was pigeons or doves, and not swallows, that flocked to us.

Meanwhile, Dad remained at home. He knew there would not be much warning if the river broke through or crested a dike. So he slept in the second-floor bedroom and attached a G.I. life raft to the roof just outside the bedroom window. Once again, army surplus proved to be useful.

Dad also felt a responsibility to other folks threatened by the rising river, David has told me. If the Columbia went rampaging on the floodplain again, Dad wanted to keep the store open as a resource for them. He and G.I. Joe's employees were prepared to sleep in the store and keep it open 24 hours a day, for as long as necessary, to offer blankets, sleeping bags, cots, stoves, and tools, including saws, and anything else that flood victims might need.

Dad could make this emergency plan because he could predict, based on his experience in the 1948 flood, that the current store at 8700 N. Vancouver Avenue would be safe and stay dry if there was another flood. That is because this G.I. Joe's was located at an even higher elevation than the precursor 1948 store had been when it had had only very shallow water incursion.

While the elevation was different, the current store was similar in an important way to the 1948 business. Both past and present G.I. Joe's were the closest general retail businesses to the Columbia floodplain in North Portland. Beleaguered residents would have looked to the store for help if there was a flood in 1956, just as the Red Cross had done eight years before during the Vanport Flood.

Thankfully, the feared flood did not materialize. Dad did not have to make a quick escape from our home's second story in the life raft, and he and others did not have to keep the store open night and day to aid flood victims.

The dikes held, and the Columbia continued coursing to the Pacific. Mom, David, and I returned home, and Dad removed the cable wrap from our house and the G.I. raft from the roof.

The only neighbors that had cleanup to do from the high water were those whose backyards were on the Columbia. While Lana Blomgren Miller remembers the fun of paddling around in a rubber raft when the river rose, she also remembers the mess it created for her dad. Then, she says, "Out came the fire hose!" Mr Blomgren cleaned up from the flooding in his backyard in 1956 just like he did from the huge flood in 1948.

Even with some folks having a little cleanup to do, what a relief it was for our community not to have to deal with a devastating flood again!

However, perhaps it was not a coincidence that Dad and Mom decided a few months later that it was time for us to move away from the floodplain and our home of five years and into a Portland suburb. ▪

Growing up with G.I. Joe's

Chapter 12

Having a Ball in the Suburbs

Portland's Madison High School in 2012, looking just as it did in 1958.

I n the summer of 1956, we moved from our home on Columbia Avenue in the country to one in a suburb on Portland's eastside. Our new home was on a ridge overlooking a city-owned golf course and was close to the soon-to-be opened Madison High School on 82nd Avenue. Madison was under construction when we moved in.

Living in the city was quite a change for my brother and me. For one thing, we now had sidewalks. I loved to ride my bike on the smooth concrete; it almost felt like I was flying! Riding in the streets was wonderful, too, and there were so many of them, compared to the few country roads to which we were accustomed.

The move made our day-to-day routine simpler, too. Gregory Heights Grade School and Madison High School were both about a block from our new home. That made our trip to school much faster and easier. When we lived at our old house, we had to walk or ride the school bus a mile to get to Columbia School. But perhaps my favorite thing about our new home's location was that there were no sloughs to walk by as we headed to our classes.

Our new neighborhood was also filled with kids, and that first summer there was so fun for us. A few kids stopped by to introduce themselves just after we moved in, and we quickly made friends, biking around in groups and playing hide-and-seek after dark.

We would gather at dusk on nearby Siskiyou Street, pick the person to be "It," and then scatter to hide in friends' and neighbors' yards. Thinking back to that time, I am amazed at how tolerant the neighbors were, with no one complaining that kids were hiding in their yards or running and shrieking, "You're It," or "Allie, Allie, alls-in-free!"

Summer ended much too soon, and we settled in to suburban life. David and I started at Gregory Heights School; Dad drove to G.I. Joe's in his red Chevy pickup, and Mom devoted herself to decorating our new home.

During the summer of 1958, just before my freshman year in high school, my brother and I hung out with our friends at Glenhaven Park. David was on a Little League team, and Mom, Dad, and I would sit in the bleachers and cheer for him. David was having trouble connecting with the baseball, despite our cheering, and that is when he discovered that he needed glasses. G.I. Joe's also sponsored a team that summer.

When David's team wound up their schedule, we watched the Rose City Little League All-Star team play. They became the Portland champs, and Mom, David, and I followed the team up to Victoria, British Columbia, to watch the play-offs there. Our team won again! They went on to Williamsport, Pennsylvania, for the Little League World Series, where they lost in the quarter-finals to an Illinois team.

How wonderful it would have been for the Rose City Little League to have gone all the way to the championship, but we were still so proud of them! Two standouts on the team went on to play in the

I was dressed up for 8th grade graduation in front of Sacramento Street home in 1958.

major leagues. According to Wikipedia, Rick Wise played 18 seasons and was a winning pitcher for the Boston Red Sox in the 1975 World Series, and Keith Lampard played nine seasons of pro baseball, including as a pinch hitter for the Houston Astros.

I am sure that the local Little League fans from that summer were not surprised at the future success of these two athletes. We knew what outstanding ball players they were, along with the rest of their teammates. ■

Growing up with G.I. Joe's

Chapter 13

The Store Grows Beyond Its Surplus Roots

*Elephants and handlers pass in front of G.I. Joe's
on way to set up circus in Delta Park, September 1957.
Photo by Charmian Orkney*

N ot only were there changes for my family, things were changing at G.I. Joe's, too. In the mid-1950s, Dad was invited to join Worldwide Distributors, based in Seattle. This buying group greatly helped surplus store owners. First, it gave them access to vendors who might not sell to individual surplus store owners, either because they were considered too small or because surplus stores were considered not to have status. Being in a buying group like Worldwide Distributors meant that owners could place large group orders, which was an incentive for suppliers to deal with them.

So Worldwide gave surplus store owners a way to start stock-

Newer concrete tilt-up portion of Store 1 in 1964, connected to older store. Note signs for photo finishing, rakes and hoes, boat cushions, fire extinguishers and bamboo fencing.

ing recognized brand-name merchandise. It also provided a way for the retailers to pay less for items because they combined all their orders to get breaks on wholesale prices.

G.I. Joe's became the tenth Worldwide Distributors' member and the first one in Oregon. Washington was home to the original nine stores, which included Bob's Surplus in nearby Longview and Yard Birds in Chehalis.

The Worldwide membership proved especially fortunate for G.I. Joe's and other Pacific Northwest surplus stores in 1960, when the army stopped auctioning most government surplus, according to my brother. The supply was cut off because of the threat of military conflict when the Soviet Union built the wall dividing East and West Berlin. With Worldwide membership,

G.I. Joe's original building, with changes, in North Portland in 1964.
Signs advertise cigarettes, bridge tokens and Levis and the slogan,
"Come in and browse around," is visible on the newer building to the left.

the store could make a switch to buying merchandise wholesale from vendors instead of from government auction.

Dad continued expanding the original store on Vancouver Avenue in North Portland. In 1960, construction doubled the square footage of the store and added a partial second floor. Dad used tilt-up construction. With that method, each wall section starts as a concrete slab poured into a frame on the ground. After all the cement slabs dry and cure, a crane lifts them into place, on to footings in the foundation.

It is a dramatic construction method because, unlike wood frame or masonry construction, you can see a concrete tilt-up building take shape in a day, when a crane lifts the walls into place.

Although Dad was planning to use the new space for retail

sales, he constructed the addition as if it were a warehouse. If the expanded retail had not been successful, he knew that he could always lease out the new building as a warehouse. He was very cautious and did not want to overextend financially.

When I was 17, I spent the summer working in that expanded store. I worked in the shoes and clothing department, helping customers, including fitting them with shoes, cashiering on the cash register, and straightening stock. I remember that shoes still needed dusting just like when I first worked in the store, so I often wore a little apron to keep the dust off my clothes.

I had wonderful bosses in shoes and clothing. Chuck Gianoli was department manager and Stan Abrams was the assistant manager. They were always pleasant and treated me like a regular employee, instead of the boss's kid.

Being the boss's kid was OK, but of course the role had its challenges. I don't recall Dad or Mom giving David and me any rules, but I do know that we were expected to work as hard as we could, definitely not to expect any special treatment, and to be polite and friendly to everyone. There was a good crew at G.I. Joe's, so most of the time it was easy to live up to expectations. Plus we knew that Dad would hear about it if we did not!

Every weekday morning that summer, Dad would take a bank deposit up Vancouver Avenue to the U.S. Bank in Walnut Park. And every morning, someone in the shoes and clothing department would call out, "How's the weather in Glocca Morra?" (The phrase was similar to the song lyrics of "How are things in Glocca Morra," from the 1947 play, *Finian's Rainbow.*) If the response came back, "The weather is great," that meant Dad was out of the store, making the deposit. Then out from under counters would come employees' coffee-filled thermoses, and everyone would pour themselves a steaming cup.

This ritual was performed with great good cheer, and I assumed it was all a game.

Dad began a policy at that time of hiring high school students to work part-time. I think these part-timers were always boys. In fact, besides me, the only high school girl I remember working at the store back then was Stan Abrams' daughter, who worked full-time in the same department I did in the summer of 1961. She was a year older than I was and getting ready to attend college. She was great company for me and I enjoyed having someone near my age to visit with on breaks.

I think that hiring high school students to work part-time was good for the company. Dad achieved some flexibility in staffing that way and was able to train the students in the store's way of doing things. A few of those part-timers stayed with the company for years and even moved into management positions as the company grew. Norm Daniels, who eventually led a buyout of the business from my brother in 1998, started working for the store part-time while he was attending Roosevelt High School.

I am sure that the students bought items from the store for themselves now and then, and I did, too. Also, when David and I were not working during the school year, Dad would sometimes bring some things home for us that he thought we might enjoy.

However, David and I did not get whatever we wanted from the store! We were raised conservatively by Dad and Mom. They had grown up during the Great Depression and wanted us to be aware of "the value of the dollar." (Even now, in my mind, I can hear Dad saying those words.)

Customers at a counter in Store 1 in the 1960s.
Photo from Worldwide Distributors

This policy was fine with David and me. I feel that my parents were fair with us; they did not get spoiled in their childhoods, and they made sure we weren't going to be either.

Dad did bring something home for me when I was in high school that I loved. It was an army surplus parka-liner that we high school girls called a "bear coat." It was made out of brownish-gray fake fur on the outside, with a rabbit-fur trimmed hood. The coat had no zipper, so you had to slip it on over your head to put it on. It fit loosely, but was so warm and cozy to wear, especially in the rain. Some girls decorated their bear coats with rickrack, but I kept mine plain.

Incidentally, I never saw the parka that the liners were supposed to fit inside of. I suspect that the government sold them in separate lots, and I don't think G.I. Joe's ever stocked them.

With Dad's focus and hard work, the store continued to grow, and in August, 1961, he incorporated G.I. Joe's. From 1961 to 1970 Dad completed the store's shift away from army surplus to general retail. G.I. Joe's ended up with a merchandise mix unique to the area that included sporting and outdoor goods, shoes and clothing, housewares, hardware, automotive and craft items, and toys.

In the mid-1960s, the store employees voted to join the Retail Clerks Union, including those working in the warehouse. During that same time period, Stores 2 and 3 were built adjacent to the original store on North Vancouver Avenue, and set a pattern for construction of the branch stores in the 1970s.

What stood out for me about my dad during this time was how much he loved the challenge of making the store the best that it could be. I remember him in the evenings when I was in high school, designing floor layouts for merchandise. He would sit on a couch in the family room with a pen and tablet, working away, while the rest of the family watched TV. It was obvious that he loved what he was doing.

As G.I. Joe's grew and expanded, David and I were growing, too, and our world was expanding beyond Portland and our family of four, or five counting the store. In 1962, I graduated from high school and went on to attend Stanford University for freshman year. I then came back and studied at Portland State College (now Portland State University) for a few years while working part time at the downtown office of freight forwarder, Tooze and Associates.

In 1964, David graduated from Madison High School and then entered the University of Oregon.

Just married! Ihsan and I cut our wedding cake

A year later, I married Ihsan Nizam, whom I had met at Portland State College. We started our life together in Syracuse, New York, and then moved to Santa Monica, California. That meant I could only follow the growth of G.I. Joe's from a distance for the next dozen or so years, until I returned to Portland in 1978. ■

Chapter 14

G.I. Joe's Goes Up Against a Fred Meyer Store

G.I. Joe's, Stores 1, 2, and 3 in 1970 in North Portland.
The original store with additions, is at top right. Photo by Hugh Ackroyd

The store really started growing in the mid-1960s when I was no longer living in Portland to witness it. Instead, my husband and I were living at the time in Southern California where he had started an electronics distributor business, and I was enjoying being a homemaker and mom. However, while my primary focus was on my new family, I still wanted to hear what was happening with the store that I had grown up with.

*Store 2 in North Portland, built in 1966 and
featuring sports and auto merchandise.*

I heard how Dad chose to build two more stores next to the
original G.I. Joe's in North Portland. Stores 2 and 3 were built
just north of the first store. Both buildings were of concrete tilt-
up construction with very high ceilings, just like the last addition to Store 1. Again, that was so they could be turned into
warehouses if the expansion did not work out well.

Store 2 was built in 1966 and featured merchandise for
sports, outdoors and autos. Store 3 was built in 1968 with a
merchandise mix of hardware, crafts and do-it-yourself items.
There was also a huge toy department for Christmas shopping.
First the toy department moved from Store 1 to Store 2, and
then, it moved on to Store 3 when that store was built.

Whenever I visited Portland, I always went out to the North
Portland stores to chat with Dad and get a tour of the latest
changes. Besides seeing Dad, I knew I might run into others to
visit with there.

Customers shop in G.I. Joe's toy department in the 1960s.
This photo is either of Store 2 or Store 3.

My husband and I, along with our baby Jamil Edward, came to Portland in 1966 to celebrate Christmas with my family. I made my trip out to the store, and, along with visiting Dad, I got to chat with my Uncle Cork (known as Roy in the store) in Store 1 and see my Granddad, who was helping out in the toy department during Christmas rush. Of course, I got to visit with Granddad at Mom's condo, too, but seeing him at the store was a bonus!

One thing I remember vividly is Dad carrying Jamil all around the original store during this Christmas trip. Dad was not very comfortable with babies and toddlers, so I was surprised that he persevered in the store tour, and especially because Jamil was nibbling on Dad's shirt collar.

In 1970, with three stores in North Portland and no more space to expand there, Dad decided it was time to build a branch store in another Portland area location. My brother was given the responsibility of finding property for the expansion.

Snow piled at side of Store No. 1
after parking lot in front of store was cleared, December, 1968.

David settled on a four-acre parcel at 184th and S.E. Stark in the Rockwood area of east Multnomah County (which was annexed to the City of Gresham in the mid-1980s). Four acres was a good-sized piece of land on which to build a branch store. There was space for the required setbacks, a parking lot, and a 50,000 square-foot building.

The real estate parcel presented a challenge, too. That was because it was across Stark Street from a Fred Meyer shopping center. Would the competition from this powerhouse grocery and general merchandise retailer prove to be too much for the proposed G.I. Joe's?

At the time, Fred Meyer was a major force in Portland. The chain was dominant in food and nonfood retail. David told me that Dad always had very high respect for Fred Meyer and its management, and often warned, "If you are going to grow retail stores in Portland, you had better learn how to compete successfully with Fred Meyer."

With that in mind, Dad told my brother it was ideal to have built-in competition from Fred Meyer for G.I. Joe's first expansion store! He said sales at the new location would let the com-

*First branch store at Rockwood, just east of Portland
in 1970, with landscaping unfinished.*

pany know right away whether they had a strong enough retail presence to go up against "Freddie's" and be OK.

So G.I. Joe's went ahead and built the Rockwood store in 1970 and then Dad had to deal with the challenge of what to sell there. He finally came up with a merchandising plan that included some product categories from all three of the original stores. And with a Fred Meyer store across the street, Dad wanted to sell merchandise categories that were not well-developed by this local retail giant. The categories he settled on included sporting goods, hunting and fishing merchandise, automotive parts and accessories, and do-it-yourself items.

The merchandise mix varied for about two years as the store slowly discontinued selling labor-intensive items, like foam rubber, plastic, and glass. These items required employee time to sell, because they were cut to size for customers.

The Rockwood store also sold boats for fishing and duck hunting, although the strong east wind coming out of the Columbia Gorge made it a challenge to display them. David told me the flat bottom boats were propped up against the front wall outside on their rear end or transom and attached to the wall with chains.

The boats would be properly displayed outside when store personnel would leave on winter evenings. But when they would return to open the store the next morning, the boats would often be tipped over, dinged up and scratched after being battered by the intense east wind during the night.

Definitely, displaying the boats outside, especially in the winter, proved to be a difficult challenge, but locating the store across from Fred Meyer was not. G.I. Joe's sales were good, and Dad got confirmation that the store would do well, even when placed close to another strong retailer.

Also in 1970, David started the first jean store for the company, having been pressured by Levi Strauss to do so. It was located in front of and connected to the original North Portland store. A contest was held for employees to choose the name for the new store, and it was won by an employee in the warehouse who submitted the name, The Pant Shop.

Two years later, David found a 12-acre parcel for sale by White Front Stores, which was a discount chain from the East Coast that had recently opened a store in Mall 205, near the 205 Freeway at S.E. Washington Street in Portland.

David determined the property would be a good location for a store. It was on McLoughlin Boulevard in Oak Grove, southeast of Portland. The challenge was that the property was larger than G.I. Joe's needed.

A solution, David suggested to Dad, was to find other businesses to buy portions of the property, and the company went ahead with the land purchase. David then sold parcels to Chevron for a gas station, to Sambo's for a restaurant and to Handyman to build a large home improvement store next to G.I. Joe's.

The design on Jean Machine bags from late 1970s through 1980s. Note old G.I. Joe's logo in center beneath far-left star.

Selling the smaller parcels recouped G.I. Joe's purchase price of the real estate. That meant their start-up expenses consisted only of the cost of store construction and inventory.

The Oak Grove store opened in 1972, and it needed more merchandise than the Rockwood store, because it was 17,500 square feet larger, with total footage of 67,500 square feet.

David then searched for property to the west of Portland and found an opportunity for G.I. Joe's to sign on as an anchor store at one end of the new Beaverton Mall on Cedar Hills Boulevard. The store covered 55,000 square feet and was the first G.I. Joe's located west of the Willamette River. It was very successful.

In 1975, G.I. Joe's decided to try an additional retail concept in the Portland area. David developed the Jean Machine store, which sold jeans and shirts, targeting teenagers and young adults as customers. The prototype store opened in the Beaverton Mall near the G.I. Joe's store. More Jean Machine stores were opened on a regular basis until there were at least 15 stores in Oregon and Washington in 1983.

David designed the store using industrial materials in intriguing ways, including creating the dressing rooms out of huge corrugated metal pipes. The pipes stood on end with a doorway cut in and the top of the pipe cut diagonally. The signature colors of the stores were turquoise, yellow, and red.

Also in 1975, G.I. Joe's started reaching out more to the community, becoming a sponsor for the Rose Cup Car Races, that took place during the Portland Rose Festival. I heard gossip that Dad initially was not too sure he wanted to sponsor the races, saying about the store, "We are not a 'blankety-blank' money tree!" Despite Dad's concern, the sponsorship worked out well because it matched the interests of a lot of the store's customers and enhanced the sale of automotive merchandise. Besides, it was good for the community.

During my Portland visits in the years between 1970 and 1975, I would still head out to Store 1 in North Portland to see Dad, because the administrative offices were there. He and I would always lunch at Waddle's at Jantzen Beach, just like my family had done when I was a kid. Usually, others would join us, and the tradition was for each of us to take out a dollar from our wallets after lunch and play liar's poker to see who would pay for the meal.

In the fall of 1976, G.I. Joe's expanded beyond Portland with the opening of a store in Salem on Lancaster Drive Northeast. The Salem store was a test, just as the first expansion store, Rockwood, had been. With Rockwood the question was whether or not G.I. Joe's could do well in a Portland area location other than North Portland. The answer was affirmative. With this new Salem store, the test was to see if the company could perform well in a city outside of Portland. The Salem store did well, and the answer was a resounding, "Yes!"

This fifth G.I. Joe's location, which was actually the seventh store, was the last one Dad opened. He passed away later that year. ■

Chapter 15

Dad's Passing

*Edward Orkney standing in front of fishing reels in Store 2.
Photo from December 1973 magazine article in* The Sporting Goods Dealer, *used with permission of the publisher, SportsOneSource, LLC*

I visited Portland shortly after the Salem G.I. Joe's opened in the fall of 1976. I came specifically to see Dad. Six months earlier, he had been diagnosed with cancer and had immediately begun a regimen of chemotherapy and radiation treatments.

I will always remember that visit with Dad, because it was the last time I saw him outside the hospital. He drove me to see the new Salem store. He was so happy with this most-recently-opened G.I. Joe's.

At the store's loading dock area, I got to see a great example of my dad in action. There was a trash compactor there, and above it was taped a handwritten sign on a piece of paper. It had an angry face drawn on it and said something like, "Put your trash in here or else!" Dad ripped it off the wall, wadded it up and tossed it in the trash. He commented, "I will not have anything negative in the store!"

We stopped in Wilsonville on the way back to Portland, so that Dad could show me the 26-acre parcel that G.I. Joe's had bought as the future site of a new distribution center. The company had just purchased the land, which was close to the I-5 Freeway. He was so proud of this purchase! He thought it was a great location from which to move merchandise, to help the company grow.

I was able to come up from my home in Southern California for one more visit with Dad later that fall when he was in St. Vincent's Hospital in Portland. That was our last time spent together.

In December, 1976, my father, Edward Orkney, passed away. He was 61 years old.

Even though Dad passed away at a relatively young age, he had lived long enough to see G.I. Joe's expand to a total of four locations in the Portland area and one in Salem. I was grateful for that. He had lived to see sales of $34 million in the last year, according to his obituary in *The Oregonian* newspaper.

I could be happy that Dad prepared for future expansion of the business with the purchase of land for a new distribution center. And I could be glad that my brother, David, had worked in the store for a number of years and was ready to take over leadership of the company.

I was grateful that my dad had been able to discover what he loved to do and was able to do it. He so cared for G.I. Joe's and the people who were a part of it! He cared for the merchandising part of the store, too, and still studied computer printouts of sales information during his last months in the hospital. Just like when he diagrammed store layouts in the early 1960s, I knew he was looking at printouts because he loved doing it.

As I wrote at the beginning of this story, when I was growing up, it was like there were five members of my family. There was Mom, Dad, my brother, me, and the store. With Dad's passing, it felt like we were now four. And while Mom and I were very supportive of that additional member of the family, G.I. Joe's, it was my brother who would take on the leadership of the store and seek to meet the continuing business challenges. ▓

Growing up with G.I. Joe's

Chapter 16

G.I. Joe's Continues to Grow and Change

David Orkney in the mid-1980s.
Photo Worldwide Distributors

My brother, David Orkney, stepped up as CEO of G.I. Joe's in late December 1976. He led the company as CEO and chairman of the board for 16 years, until 1992 and then continued on as board chairman only, for another six years. During that time, new stores were

Crane raising walls of distribution center in Wilsonville in 1978 or early 1979.

opened throughout Oregon and into Washington, including in the Seattle/Tacoma area.

Construction on the distribution center that Dad and David had envisioned in 1976 was started in 1978 on part of the 26-acre parcel in Wilsonville, Oregon. It was like a celebration the day that a huge crane lifted up the facility's precast concrete walls and set them in their footings around the foundation. Mom and I, along with my kids, Jamil, Sam, and Laurie, joined David and others at the construction site to watch the distribution center take shape.

In one day, the building went from foundation, with pre-cast walls lying on the ground, to looking like a building with the walls in place. Of course, it was missing a roof, but the structure still looked like a building. I had never watched a tilt-up building being raised up before, and found the process quite amazing.

Late in 1978 was when I started working for the store again. G.I. Joe's Box Office premiered in the Portland area locations early in 1979, and I joined the company to set up and manage the ticket outlet system prior to the opening.

Also in 1979, The 104,000 square-foot distribution center was completed and opened for merchandise. Approximately 50 people worked there, most coming from the North Portland facility.

More openings happened in 1979, with G.I. Joe's starting up two more stores, one in the Portland area and one in Bend, Oregon. The Portland store was G.I. Joe's second store in the suburbs of southeast Portland, and was also the second store to serve as a mall anchor.

The anchor store was 60,000 square feet and located in Eastport Plaza on 82nd Avenue. The new, smaller Bend store was in a smaller mall. Management planned to have this 35,000-square-foot branch serve as a prototype for expansion stores they planned to open in smaller cities in Oregon.

A few years later, 1982 proved to be a big year for the company. The original G.I. Joe's Store 1 closed, as did adjacent Stores 2 and 3. The Delta Park G.I. Joe's took the place of all three. This store, one-quarter mile from the old trio of stores, was still convenient for customers in North Portland and Vancouver, Washington, and the new store was attractive with an updated, cleaner look.

New Box Office sign in Beaverton store early in 1979 draws attention to the ticket sales counter at the front of the store.

When Store 1 closed, the old administrative office closed as well. The office had been located on the second floor, up a long stairway off the loading dock. With the closure, management moved into the newly constructed corporate headquarters, which was built next to the distribution center in Wilsonville.

The new, 20,000-square-foot office building was light and airy and had a modern design. It was a stark contrast to the basically makeshift old environment of small, windowless offices.

I think the new office was symbolic of G.I. Joe's growth into a recognized Pacific Northwest retailer, but one that could still have fun. There was quirky art on the walls to show that dedication to fun. After all, the store's message to customers was still to get out and enjoy the outdoors, or do-it-yourself projects, like fixing cars or growing gardens. It just wouldn't do to have offices that looked formal and stuffy!

Also, it was practical and efficient to have the administrative and buying office adjacent to the warehouse, so that buyers could check on incoming shipments and inventory.

With the move, G.I. Joe's instigated a policy for the buyers to walk through the distribution center twice a day to monitor stock arrival and out-flow. David told me that "Retail is all about distribution and that function is a key ingredient in assuring full stores with no empty shelves." Keeping close track of inventory "is especially important," David said, when a store has "a high amount of advertised merchandise," as G.I. Joe's did, starting in the 1970s.

Of course, bar codes and computerized data eventually became the main way to track merchandise flow for retail business, beginning in the early 1990s. However, prior to that time, walking the warehouse floor was the best way for G.I. Joe's buyers to make sure that items had arrived from vendors for an upcoming sale. And they could also expedite the transfer of merchandise to stores that needed it.

Growth continued, and between 1983 and January, 31, 1990, six additional stores were opened. The company decided to narrow its focus, and the Jean Machine stores were sold during this time, according to G.I. Joe's financial statements. ■

Growing up with G.I. Joe's

Chapter 17

My Brother
Scouts for Real Estate

*The Oak Grove store south of Portland opened in 1972 and
had a large, free-standing sign with an announcement board.*

We all know how crucial a store's location is to its success. For instance, when I am going shopping, I take into consideration how close a store is to me, how easy it is to get to, and if there is good access to it from a parking lot or from a mall.

Choosing good locations for new G.I. Joe's stores was what my brother, David Orkney, did for over twenty years. From 1970 until 1991, he found the right parcel of real estate to build a new store on, or a good mall leasing opportunity for 15 G.I. Joe's expansion stores (David found two locations in East Multnomah County, because the Rockwood store was closed and replaced by a branch in Gresham's Town Fair mall in 1987). He also found and managed the purchase of the land for the store's distribution center and administrative office in Wilsonville, south of Portland.

David's concentration on real estate started in 1970, when he agreed with Dad that it was time to expand the company beyond the three stores in North Portland.

They chose to go with a "ring-around Portland" plan, and David started looking for real estate to the east, west, and south of the city. Stores in those areas would complete the ring, since G.I. Joe's was already located in the north.

As related in Chapter 14, David decided that a four-acre parcel in Rockwood would be the best place to build the first expansion store. Dad liked the location, too, and so David negotiated the land purchase. He then changed hats and worked as construction manager for G.I. Joe's, working with Allen McMillan, who built the store as general contractor.

So, when it was completed, Dad and David had their eastern store in the ring. The property David found and bought two years later, was in Oak Grove on McLoughlin Boulevard. It became the site for the G.I. Joe's south of Portland. Again, the company built the store, with Allen McMillan as general contractor and David as construction manager.

In another two years, in 1974, David found an opportunity for the store to become an anchor in the Beaverton Mall (now named Cedar Hills Crossing). The C.E. John Company of Vancouver, Washington, was the builder and owner of the new mall, and David signed on for G.I. Joe's to be a part of it. This store to the west of Portland completed the first "ring around Portland" for G.I. Joe's.

Then, David found a real estate parcel in Salem for a free-

Salem Store in 1976, with a simplified exterior design.

standing store. Dad gave the OK to buy it, and again Allen McMillan was the general contractor with David working as project manager. This first store out of the Portland area opened in the fall of 1976. It was located to the east of the I-5 Freeway on Lancaster Drive, N.E., and the zoning code allowed G.I. Joe's to build a store of 62,000 square feet.

Earlier in 1976, G.I. Joe's had bought land in Wilsonville for the new distribution center and a new administrative office. David found that property, too.

Currently, Wilsonville's strategic location for distribution throughout the Portland area is well known, but that wasn't the case when G.I. Joe's first purchased the land. Back then, David says, Wilsonville had yet to be discovered as a prime distribution point.

David had started searching for a distribution center site because G.I. Joe's had outgrown the warehouse they were leasing in North Portland, near the original store.

Since the six stores were located in a ring around Portland, with the Salem store to come soon, David could look throughout the Portland Metro area for a site. One requirement that Dad and David had was that there be railroad tracks nearby, so that the company could have a spur for deliveries by rail.

At the time, G.I. Joe's was receiving 15 to 20 rail cars a year of merchandise. David told me that these deliveries really cut store costs, compared to truck deliveries. Also, in 1976, holding up to a two-year supply of key merchandise was better economically than relying on periodic truck deliveries.

(Incidentally, in later years, as the economy changed and financing costs went up, it became too costly for the store to carry large inventories of merchandise, and the company returned to receiving most of its deliveries by truck, ordered by buyers as needed. In the early 1990s, my brother says that rail deliveries were down to the equivalent of three to five cars per year.)

David got started on his property search for a distribution center and checked out a warehouse facility that Payless Drug Stores was selling in the Beaverton area. It looked good and had the requisite rail connection.

Then, he heard of 26 acres of farmland for sale in Wilsonville and checked it out. The parcel met the requirement of being close to railroad tracks, and G.I. Joe's could build a rail spur to connect to them.

The Wilsonville property was cheaper than the Beaverton warehouse, at 25 cents per square foot, or $11,000 per acre. That was good, but perhaps the most important question was: How efficient a location would it be for moving merchandise throughout the Portland area and to the new Salem store?

To find out, Dad and David divided up the stores. Dad chose

to drive to a few from Wilsonville, and David drove to the rest. They checked mileage and how long it took to make their trips. Then, they conducted the same informal test, driving from the available Beaverton warehouse to all the stores.

The Wilsonville property won the driving tests! The property had the advantage of being adjacent to I-5 Freeway and very near the connection to the I-205 Freeway. That compared to Beaverton's connection with the smaller and more congested Highway 217 and the Sunset Highway.

G.I. Joe's went ahead and bought the Wilsonville acreage, and within six months, Payless Drug followed the store's lead, buying property there to build a warehouse. However, by then, the cost per acre had gone up four times, from 25 cents per square foot to $1. per square foot.

The timing of the Wilsonville land purchase was ideal for G.I. Joe's, because an important part of the I-205 Freeway near Wilsonville had just been completed in 1975. The freeway then ran almost 18 miles between the nearby Tualatin interchange on the I-5 Freeway to Sunnyside in east Multnomah County.

G.I. Joe's bought the property shortly after that portion of the freeway opened, and it seems that the improvement in transportation movement for the Portland Metro area had not yet been factored in to the land prices in Wilsonville

So, G.I. Joe's benefited from luck, as well as careful research by my brother and father, in the timing of their distribution center land purchase. It just happened that the lease on their North Portland warehouse was expiring at a time when the new freeway made Wilsonville an attractive place to locate, but before land prices reflected that.

And looking ahead, the warehouse's Wilsonville location

became potentially even more advantageous for the company in 1983 when the last portion of the I-205 Freeway was finished in East Portland. That, combined with the opening of the Glenn L. Jackson Bridge over the Columbia River a year earlier, presented a convenient freeway connection for G.I. Joe's to eventually move merchandise between Wilsonville and Vancouver, Washington, and on north as the company expanded further into Washington state. ■

Chapter 18

David Orkney, CEO and Real Estate Point Man

David talks with employees at orientation meeting before opening of new Eugene store in March 1983. David's photo, given to him by Don Nelsen of Olympic Tool.

D avid did the footwork to find good property for G.I. Joe's expansion, but sometimes opportunities for a store location were just presented to him because of business relationships which had developed with the business expansion. These opportunities were not due to luck, as mentioned in the last chapter, but to honest and reliable dealings with others.

Even so, it wasn't always easy to have good business relationships with real estate principals. According to David, G.I. Joe's and the C.E. John Company, developer of the Beaverton Mall, had a conflict during their first year of the Beaverton store's lease over how to interpret some payment terms in the lease contract. The dispute eventually went to court and was settled in G.I. Joe's favor.

The judge's ruling ended the disagreement, and there were no hard feelings on either side. In fact, a friendly business relationship between the two companies continued on, even better than it had been originally.

David speaks with great respect for owner Clint John, who was a contemporary of Dad's and started his company, C.E. John, building homes after World War II. The business grew and developed several large shopping centers in the Pacific Northwest and continues on today. My brother says that Mr. John "was from the same mold as Dad," and a handshake would seal a deal.

After the trial, David reported that, Mr. John said, "Well, I guess you were right after all. I thought you were wrong." Then he shook David's hand, demonstrating his old-time courtesy and willingness to move on.

This mutual respect between the two companies led to G.I. Joe's being welcomed into C.E. John's Mountain View Mall development in Bend, Oregon. This was G.I. Joe's second store outside the Portland area and it opened in 1979.

Then, also in 1979, as mentiond previously, G.I. Joe's added to the stores circling the Portland area with the opening of a branch in Eastport Plaza, a well-established neighborhood mall in a suburb of southeast Portland.

G.I. Joe's expansion focus then returned to the I-5 Freeway corridor in Oregon, starting with the opening of a new Delta Park store in North Portland in 1982. This store replaced the three original North Portland stores and they were closed. Concurrently, the administrative offices were moved from Store 1 to G.I. Joe's newly constructed headquarters in Wilsonville. The following year, a branch store opened in Eugene, Oregon, along the I-5 corridor, as well.

Looking for another expansion site, David found a large parcel of land at the Tualatin/Lake Grove exit of the I-5 Freeway, south of Portland. He liked it, saying it "short-stopped" Lake Oswego traffic getting on the I-5. However, the site was too large for G.I. Joe's to buy on its own, so David approached Payless Drugs to see if they wanted to go in on the deal, with the two companies each anchoring one end of the mall. Payless declined. However, then the landlord signed Safeway to anchor the mall at one end, and G.I. Joe's went ahead with building the anchor store at the other end.

The Tualatin store opened in October, 1985. A month later, Vice President Norm Daniels was quoted in *The Oregonian* saying that this newest store had the third highest sales out of G.I. Joe's ten stores. That sales figure proved again how important location was in the siting of a store. And it was something that David seemed to understand intuitively, giving him the assurance to go with properties that others might not initially see as attractive.

The Tualatin store was the last one for which David provided the construction management. It finally made sense to turn that job over to Wayne Jackson, head of the finance department.

But David continued locating properties for the store's growth. The Medford store in southern Oregon opened in 1986, and the distribution center was expanded to keep up with the additional stores. In 1987, G.I. Joe's opened a store in a Gresham mall, which replaced the first branch store in Rockwood.

The first Washington state store was opened in Vancouver, close to the I-205 Freeway in 1989. That was followed by a new store in Albany, Oregon, again along the I-5 corridor.

In 1991, David found his fifteenth property for a store and the second site for one in Washington state. It was located in Federal Way and was the first branch in the Seattle/Tacoma area. Again, it was near the I-5 Freeway, for ease of distribution.

In 1992, David stepped down as CEO and real estate point man for the company, while remaining as majority stockholder and G.I. Joe's chairman of the board of directors. With his 22 years of concentrating on store real estate, he left the business a legacy of great store locations and an outstanding site for G.I. Joe's distribution center and administration office.

I wanted to write this chapter because my brother is so low-key and modest. Like Dad taught us, David doesn't brag or even talk of his accomplishments. Only when I began asking him questions about the chain's growth, did I discover these contributions of David's to G.I. Joe's success, that go along the other contributions he made as company CEO.

Sometimes, I think we all have an unconscious belief that an executive has to be unpleasant and dictatorial to be effective. Not true! David certainly does not fit that description. He is likeable, with a slightly wry sense of humor—someone you might think could have been president of his high school class.

Well, in David's case, he was, and twice! He was president of both his freshman class and senior class.

So my brother didn't fit a boss stereotype when he was running G.I. Joe's, and I am so glad he didn't. Yes, he was the boss and he made tough decisions, but he also was approachable and, after a conversation with him, you probably would be laughing at one of his jokes.

I remember one Christmas when I worked at the store and David was wearing a red sweater with a big, white *C* on the front. I asked him what it was for. He said, "It is a *C* for Christmas." I thought that unusual, but it still made sense.

Then, just the other day, I asked him about his red Christmas sweater. He said, "Oh, yeah, but that was the sweater I also wore when we were preparing our yearly budget. Then, the *C* stood for cash flow."

That's my brother! Just when I think I have him figured out, there is always something else to learn! ▪

Growing up with G.I. Joe's

Chapter 19

The Box Office is My Ticket Back to G.I. Joe's

The sign company rep joined me at the sign installation at Beaverton G.I.Joe's Box Office in 1979.

returned to the Portland area with my three children in 1978, after my divorce. I wanted to make a contribution to G.I. Joe's and my brother offered me the job of setting up and managing a new department selling event tickets. We named it the Box Office.

The new ticket outlet system was a partnership between G.I.

*The Box Office staff toured Portland Civic Stadium in 1979,
prior to the opening of the ticket outlets.
Tom Lasley of Thunder Media, third from right, and yes, it was chilly!*

Joe's and Thunder Media, and I think it worked well for both of us. Thunder Media was owned by Mike Nealy, who promoted rock concerts and car races and, as of this writing, owns Global Events Group. Tom Lasley, who had previously supplied tickets for a ticket outlet in Meier and Frank's large department store in downtown Portland, started the ticket sales business for Thunder Media, and I worked with him.

Tom obtained tickets for entertainment and sports events, and we sold them at five of the Portland area stores and sometimes in the Salem store. The Box Office also sold tickets that were directly provided to us, since G.I. Joe's was a sponsor for events like car races and local college football and basketball games.

It was my job to design and set up the ticket offices in all the Portland stores. G.I. Joe's, at the time, had a great carpentry department, and I enjoyed working with Jimmy Rose to get just the right look and features for our offices.

Each sales area included a counter with storage drawers for tickets, a display area, an overhead sign, as well as a round kiosk for putting up posters. Of course, I went with the store colors of red and blue, but the blue was more a Columbia blue than navy. The red and blue ended up matching the colors of my old high school, Madison, but that was just a coincidence.

Next, it was time to hire staff to sell the tickets. G.I. Joe's management wanted Box Office personnel to be knowledgeable about seating in the major Portland venues in order to share that with customers, and also to have information about the performances and sports events for which we sold tickets. That is why the Box Office was a separate department with its own staff.

After I hired everybody, Tom Lasley arranged a field trip for us to visit Portland Civic Stadium and Auditorium, and the Memorial Coliseum. We toured the facilities and talked to staff at each location, so that everyone at the Box Office would be ready to help customers make good seating choices.

Selling tickets in the stores was a winning idea. G.I. Joe's covered the whole Portland metro area with the five stores. There was the original store in North Portland, the southeast Portland area store in Oak Grove, the one east of Portland in the Rockwood community, one in southeast Portland at Eastport Plaza, and also one west of the city in Beaverton.

On the mornings that tickets would go on sale for a hot rock concert, teenagers would line up outside the front doors of the stores, with these lines wrapping around to the side of the buildings. I think it surprised a few of the store managers the first few times they arrived to open their stores and found a crowd waiting for them!

But we carefully planned the ticket sales for groups like Van

One of the Box Office's great staff members ready to help customers.

Halen or REO Speedwagon in advance. All the ticket outlets were stocked with the concert tickets, and staff members diagrammed the seating chart ahead of time, so that when the customers rushed to the ticket counter, everything was ready to go.

Of course, Tom Lasley and I thrived on the excitement generated by the sale of tickets for these top rock and roll concerts. And having the lines of eager ticket buyers created good publicity for the Box Office both in and out of the company.

Back then, G.I. Joe's ticket selling was conducted totally as a community service. We did not even levy a service charge, which would be very unusual today. We also placed the Box Office in the very front of the store, which was, of course, a prime spot for selling anything! Tom and I were so pleased that my brother and the management team recognized that this placement created customer goodwill, because a ticket buyer did not have to walk through other sales departments trying to find the Box Office. Other ticket outlets might use that strategy with the goal of selling merchandise as an impulse purchase, but G.I. Joe's wanted to focus on customer service.

In addition to touring events like rock concerts or classical music and dance performances, we promoted local college athletics, selling sports tickets for both Portland State University and University of Portland. Customers could also buy tickets for local community events, like the Molalla Buckeroo rodeo. And of course, we sold tickets for the car races G.I. Joe's sponsored, like the Rose Cup and Grand Prix. The ticket booth was the place in the store to buy hunting and fishing licenses, too.

The Box Office made it easy for Portlanders to buy tickets, no matter where they lived, so it was good for customers. It was good for G.I. Joe's, too, because it brought new shoppers into the stores. The store really benefited when there was an event refund, since this was in the days before ATM machines. A cash refund for an event would put money in the hands of someone who might then decide to spend it on the spot!

I also gathered a lot of information about what events were popular in different parts of town. One of the challenges for me, in that time before computers, was to determine how to distribute the tickets among the stores. The challenge was to forecast demand at the different locations and divide them up accordingly. I got to be pretty good at it.

As I recall, the data showed what a Portlander could probably predict. I learned that folks living on the eastside rocked out, and that folks on the westside flocked to cultural events. I wish I had been able to discover how to put this information to use back then, since this was a pre-Google, pre-search-engine time, and nobody else had these figures.

I also learned a lot about events, but it took a while. I remember the first time I took one of my kids to a concert. We went to see Jethro Tull, and I was shocked when security personnel searched my bag as we entered the Memorial Coliseum. I wasn't expecting that because I had never attended a concert before! We didn't even end up liking Jethro Tull's music and left early to get some ice cream at a shop near home.

I met Charlie Daniels at the Rockwood Store, where he was promoting his upcoming concert and records.

The only time I got a backstage pass at the Coliseum was for a Village People concert. Now why couldn't it have been a backstage pass for a Bee Gees concert or for Jackson Browne? Anyway, it was not exciting backstage, so I headed for my seat, where I enjoyed the energetic concert.

My time at the Box Office was interesting while it lasted, and I was fortunate to be working with Tom Lasley. He was kind, competent, smart, and always upbeat. We laughed a lot in the course of taking care of tickets and promoting events for our customers. One of his jokes was that there was going to be a 10-point pop quiz on whatever we were working on.

He was a character, too, and you could tell by the way he

dressed. Tom was probably in his early 30s when we started the Box Office, and he would usually stroll into my office wearing khaki pants, a letterman's jacket of some kind, and saddle shoes or athletic shoes. That was pretty much his uniform and it worked for him.

Tom went on to head up the Ticketmaster business in Portland, establishing that in 1987. His outlets for Ticketmaster continued to be located in G.I. Joe's stores, just like those of the Box Office, and there was also an outlet in the Jean Machine store at the Portland Galleria.

I was sorry to hear of Tom's passing in March 2014, just as I was winding up writing this book. He was one of the good guys and I know he will be missed by many, including me.

I met many other wonderful people in and out of G.I. Joe's during this time. That included the staff members of the Box Office at the five stores, who were outstanding. They helped customers find the best seats, kept track of what seats we sold, and managed all the supply of tickets for many events at the same time.

In the job, I also gained skills as a manager. My previous work experience, other than G.I. Joe's, had consisted of working as a secretary or bookkeeper in various offices. These included working for freight forwarder, Tooze and Associates in Portland, and for an architect's office, a steel fabrication plant, and an ad agency in Los Angeles. I was happy to step up to management with the ticket outlet system.

My office, along with everyone else working in the central administrative office, was on the second floor of Store 1 in North Portland. My desk was in the advertising office, with Lynn Studer, Barbara Patterson, and others, and our wild jungle wallpaper livened up the atmosphere. Our office was situated next to the office of Norm Daniels, who was my boss. A lot of conversation went on in our office, but we got our work done, too. I also loved to visit with Kaye McMillan May who ran the sign shop, whenever I stopped in there to make some promo materials for the Box Office.

However, my time working with the ticket outlets came to an end in the spring of 1980. That is when management decided that the Box Office would become a department in the individual stores, instead of one separate department with me as its manager. So, I left G.I. Joe's and was never so directly involved with the store again. ■

Chapter 20

Changing the Merchandise Mix to Gain a Competitive Edge

Marine Department when store still sold boats, like at left.
Photo probably of Oak Grove store in 1970s.

Just as finding great locations for the stores was important for G.I. Joe's success, so was selling products shoppers wanted at prices that were attractive to them. It was also important that the stores had a retail identity strong enough to draw customers in the doors. And needless to say, the mix of products sold contributed hugely to G.I. Joe's retail identity.

The decade of the 1980s was definitely a time when management sharpened G.I Joe's product mix. Retail competition dramatically increased throughout that decade, with more stores competing with G.I. Joe's in a variety of product categories. While the family business was adding new branches, national chain stores with low prices and some similar merchandise, like Target and Wal-Mart, were moving into the Pacific Northwest.

Also adding stores in the Portland area were Pacific Northwest stores, REI, and Eddie Bauer, both of which competed with G.I. Joe's in some merchandise categories. Another competitor, Northwest-based, big box retailer Costco, built stores in Oregon, as well. It offered some competition to the store, but not on a regular basis, since Costco's merchandise mix varied.

In light of the increasing retail competition, David and his board were faced with the hard question of what product categories would be most advantageous for G.I. Joe's to sell and what categories it would be wise to downplay or eliminate. Aiding in this decision-making process were their observations of what the national chains were selling and what they were not. That led to the question of what merchandise and departments the store could emphasize that the national retailers overlooked.

In the 1980s, the G.I. Joe's team decided that the company should begin moving away from selling general merchandise, including housewares, small electronics, plants and garden items. That would lessen their direct competition with general retailers like Target, Wal-Mart, and even Northwest retail giant, Fred Meyer. Management decided this was a first step in tightening the merchandise focus while they considered what product categories to build up.

The decision was also made to stop selling boats. That would

Tent platform, probably in Oak Grove store in the 1970s.

eliminate some competition with marine specialty retailers and also free up a lot of sales space because of the large size of boats compared to other merchandise.

So, the store's merchandise mix was narrowed, and G.I. Joe's management eventually decided to focus on what they sold best and leave the rest. The prototype for G.I. Joe's new direction was presented to customers with the opening of the second Washington state branch in 1991, which was located in Federal Way, between Seattle and Tacoma.

This new store targeted sporting goods, and outdoor recreation and automotive merchandise. The redefined product mix was summed up with G.I. Joe's new tagline, "Sports and Automotive."

The Federal Way store presented the model for changes to the existing stores in Oregon and Vancouver, Washington. Management planned to systematically transform these stores in a period of five years, from 1993 to 1998. Not only was the transformation to include the new sporting goods, outdoor and automotive merchandise emphasis, but also the plan was to improve the stores' layouts and design.

With this new merchandising plan and anticipated store upgrades, came a change of company leadership, as well. In 1992, after serving as CEO for 16 years, David handed over the CEO duties to longtime employee, Norm Daniels. It was decided that Norm, in his new position, could better direct the changes in the stores and in the product mix. Norm had served as Vice President for marketing for many years prior to this change.

And although no longer CEO, David continued on as chairman of the board of directors of G.I. Joe's.

Then, in 1998, Norm Daniels led a buyout of the business and took over as chairman of the board and majority owner of G.I. Joe's. When David sold his majority interest in the business to Norm and his financial partners, there were 14 stores in Oregon and Washington.

And so, G.I. Joe's continued on with new leadership and carried with it my family's best wishes and hopes for success. David still served on the board of directors, looking at the big picture for the company, but he was no longer active in its day-to-day business. ■

Chapter 21

New Owners Instigate Change, Rapid Growth and then Fail

Norm Daniels and his financial partners owned G.I. Joe's from 1998 to 2007 and several more stores were opened during that time.

A 12-page newspaper insert celebrating G.I. Joe's 50 years in business appeared in 2002 in *The Oregonian* and also in a Seattle paper, and maybe others. This section listed 18 G.I. Joe's stores and announced that two more would open that year.

Five years later, in 2007, Norm Daniels and his partners sold the company to San Francisco-based Gryphon Investors, although Norm stayed on as CEO. With the change in ownership came a change in the name. Even though the business had thrived as G.I. Joe's for 55 years, the new management decided it was time for a change. The name they came up with was Joe's Sports, Outdoor and More.

I believe that the removal of the "G.I." from the beginning of the store name was deeply symbolic and it demonstrated that the new owners did not understand how deep G.I. Joe's roots were in Oregon and possibly the whole Pacific Northwest. Customers understood how the name was tied to those roots, but the new top management did not. And if they did not understand how important the name was, what else didn't they understand?

The name change surprised me. If the name had been good

enough for so many years, why change it? And what message did removing the "G.I." send to anyone who had served or was serving in the armed forces?

It was a bad move, I believe. I can only assume that by calling the company Joe's, the management was trying to make the store more generic and hoping to appeal to a larger buyout firm in a few years. I think their goal was to remove anything from the store that made it unique, so that it could be just another sporting goods store, shaped from the same cookie cutter as all the others.

And the name Gryphon chose was not good. When I first heard the name, Joe's Sports, Outdoor and More, I wondered why *Outdoor* was not plural, when *Sports* was. Plus, whenever I hear *More* in a business name, it seems to me the owners don't have a good handle on what they are selling. If store owners can't define their merchandise, sticking *More* in the name doesn't clarify to customers what they will find on the store's shelves and racks when they shop.

Of course, the business continued, whether I liked the new name or not. In 2008, the leadership of Joe's Sports, Outdoor and More changed further, and Norm Daniels was replaced as CEO by Hal Smith, who was a former CEO of Bass Pro Shops. The company rapidly expanded, but was burdened by heavy debt related to the 2007 buyout.

In July, 2008, the company listed 28 stores on their old website, www.gijoes.com. These included 14 Oregon stores: Albany, Bend, Beaverton, Delta Park, Eugene, Gresham, Hillsboro, Johnson Creek, Medford, Oak Grove, Salem on Lancaster Drive NE, Salem on Commercial Street, Sherwood, and Tualatin.   *

Eight of the Oregon stores were in the extended Portland area: Beaverton, Delta Park, Gresham, Hillsboro, Johnson Creek, Oak Grove, Sherwood, and Tualatin.

By 2008, the chain also included 14 Washington stores: Bellingham, Federal Way, Issaquah, Kennewick, Kent, Kirkland, Lake Stevens, Lakewood, Lynnwood, Mt. Vernon, Puyallup, Seattle, Spokane Valley, and Vancouver. Eight of the Washington stores were in the extended Seattle-Tacoma area: Federal Way, Issaquah, Kent, Kirkland, Lakewood, Lynnwood, Puyallup, and Seattle.

Three more stores were added after I looked at the summer 2008 website, including two stores in Idaho. They were located in Nampa and nearby Meridian, and it was the first time the G.I. Joe's or Joe's Sports chain had opened stores in the state. The third new store was in Washington state, in Renton.

Unexpectedly after such rapid expansion, the G.I. Joe's story ended abruptly the next year. Joe's Sports, Outdoor and More filed a Chapter 11 bankruptcy in March 2009. According to the terms of the bankruptcy, the business had one month to find a buyer. No buyer came forward and the company liquidation started in April 2009.

A longtime Pacific Northwest business was closing, just two years after investors from outside the region bought it. According to an article in *The Oregonian*, 31 Joe's Sports, Outdoor and More stores closed their doors forever, and 1,600 employees lost their jobs.

The suddenness of liquidation after the store declared bankruptcy was mind-boggling to me. It only took a month for a 57-year-old business to go under. I wasn't there, so I don't know exactly what happened, but I do believe the contents of a May 29, 2009 article from *The Oregonian* that was published with the headline, "Joe's Demise Didn't Have to Happen."

Of course, it did happen; the story is over, and it doesn't matter why at this point.

But I am still saddened by it.

I think back to my father, Edward Orkney, and how his main focus after leaving the Army Air Forces in 1945 was to build a business. His goal had not been to grow G.I. Joe's fast and then find someone to buy him out for big bucks.

Dad was challenged to create something solid that could continue to provide security to employees and serve as a resource for the larger community even after he was gone. Money and possessions did not seem to interest him much. Dad did not invest in property for himself or buy fancy houses or cars. What he focused on was building the business, pure and simple, and I think it took that singleness of vision to accomplish what he did.

While G.I. Joe's is no more, I do think back, now and then, to my first involvement with the store all those years ago. I think of the fun times, when G.I. Joe's sold mostly army surplus. I think of when it was my job to "neaten" the bins and it was David's job to clean off the Cosmoline from small machine parts. We had a good time while working, but, sorry, David, I think I got the better job! ▪

Chapter 22

G.I. Joe's People

Dad and Bob Ollerenshaw in photo for December 1973 article in a national magazine, The Sporting Goods Dealer. *Used with permission from publisher, SportsOneSource, LLC.*

My father always attracted good folks to work at G.I. Joe's. Men such as Art Bruer, David Haag, Curt Reynolds, Stuart Richmond, Bob Ollerenshaw, Clarence "Smitty" Smith, and Chuck Gianoli started working at the store in the 1950s and 1960s and continued as the business grew. These were good people who also had the courtesy to take the time to answer a question from the little kid I was back then.

Another person I remember from the early, early days is Florence Johansen; she made an amazing walnut torte for Christmas, and I got to have some!

Stuart Richmond shines in my memory, too. When David and I were teenagers working at the store in the summer, Stu would sometimes take us to work and back when Dad was in Seattle attending Worldwide Distributors meetings. I didn't think much about it at the time, but now think how nice it was of him. He probably would have much preferred a quiet commute to work, without two teenagers tagging along.

My brother recently reminded me that Art Bruer was Dad's second-in-command pretty much from the beginning until 1974 when Art retired. David praised Art for being so ethical and conscientious and always being willing to give employees another chance when they made a mistake. David knew Art better than I did because he worked with him as a colleague. But I do remember him always being in the store during my childhood visits there. As an adult, my clearest memories of Art are of him being so busy and always hurrying from one department or store to another with a list in his hand!

Others I recall who joined the company early, from the 1960s on, include Herb Jundt, Claude McCuwen, Betty Menconi, Ben Mallery, Barbara Mallery, Kaye McMillan Synoground, Lynn Studer, Debbie Brown Uilenberg, Jimmy Rose, Tom May, Duane Mellon, Wayne Jackson, and Brian Sieler, plus all the other Portland-area store managers and buyers.

The Menconi family would probably take the award for the highest number of family members working at the store, if there was one. Betty Menconi was the longtime head of personnel, and her sons, Ron and Mike, joined the company. Then, Ron married Debbie and Mike married Mary Ann, making a grand total of five family members at G.I. Joe's, and, this doesn't even count extended family through the two marriages!

Bob Ollerenshaw's two sons, Bruce and Gary, also joined their dad at the store. Bruce became an automotive buyer and Gary became a store manager. Then, there was Allen McMillan who was the general contractor for the construction of many of the G.I. Joe's stores. His daughter, Kaye, with whom I liked to visit, was head of the sign shop that produced company advertising and graphics when I worked at the Box Office.

Bill Brown came to work at G.I. Joe's after owning a surplus store in Vancouver, and he was joined by his daughter, Debbie. Hers was the distinctive, smooth voice of G.I. Joe's when people called the administrative office. She also greeted and directed vendor salespeople to the right merchandise buyers. And one of those buyers was Debbie's husband, Dirk Uilenberg.

B.G. Eilertson, who eventually became Sporting Goods Merchandise Manager, started working for the store when he was 16 years old. He joined his mother, Adelle, who was a cashier in the automotive section, and was so petite that she would stand on a case of motor oil to operate the cash register.

Dad also liked to hire high school kids to work part-time. He hired students mainly from Jefferson High School, because the original stores were in the Jefferson school district, and from Madison High School, which David and I attended.

Claude McCuwen and also Herb Jundt, who became the automotive buyer, attended Jefferson and worked for G.I. Joe's for a while. And Larry Forsythe, who attended Columbia School and was in my fourth-grade class, also worked at the store. My former classmate had played on the football team at Jefferson and, legend has it that he liked to chase shoplifters after they took merchandise out the door, perhaps even tackling them at the end of his pursuit!

I am still finding out, even now, about friends who worked for a while at the store when they were young. At my 50th Madison High reunion in September 2012, John Elliott, a friend and classmate, told me he worked at G.I. Joe's for a summer before heading back to college. That was news to me! One of his jobs had been cleaning Cosmoline off of engine parts using diesel oil, just like my brother had done.

Some other Madison students who worked briefly at G.I. Joe's include Steve Dunn, and brothers, Kent and Mike MacIntosh. The Madison wrestling team was well-represented, as these classmates were on the team along with my brother. Ben Mallery also attended Madison, and grew with the company, joining the board of directors for a time. And his wife, Barbara Mallery, was head of the accounting department.

These stories show that Portland was a small town in many ways. That was demonstrated to me when I attended the first fancy G.I. Joe's stockholders' dinner in 1975 at the Red Lion Inn at Jantzen Beach/Hayden Island. The event was very special for my dad, and he invited me to come up to Portland from my home in Southern California to attend.

I got all dressed up in a floor-length, forest-green dress, and then Dad picked me up to take me to the event. I think Dad was so proud to put on this dinner for stockholders, who were also G.I. Joe's employees, because it was a "thank you" to them for all their contributions to the company's success.

And who did I see there but Ray Van Beek, who was then the store's chief financial officer and someone I had known in high school. I had met Ray, who attended Washington High School, through Richard Thompson who also went to Washington and whom I dated when I was a high school senior.

This is just another example of how the company still had a neighborly feel to it in the mid-1970s, in spite of its growth and the growth of Portland.

In looking back, I regret that I cannot even begin to mention all the wonderful people who worked for the store over the years. And of course, I focus on folks from the early times, when I was most involved with the business.

While I didn't know all the employees, especially from the later years, there is one thing I do know. It took everyone's contribution to build G.I. Joe's, and I am happy to have shared in that with all those who worked so hard over the years. ■

Growing up with G.I. Joe's

Chapter 23

Wigs to Waterbeds and Rock Tumblers, Too

Shoppers in Store 1 prior to 1970 when cigarette sales discontinued. Photo from Worldwide Distributors

Because G.I. Joe's went through so many phases during its 57-year run, I think almost every conceivable kind of merchandise was sold at the store at one time or another, except groceries, although some food items were offered. In the original store, candy and popcorn were for sale some of the time in the early years, as well as ice cream cones.

During G.I. Joe's war surplus era, from 1952 through the early 1960s, the store carried a wide and somewhat unpredictable variety of merchandise. In addition to items like knapsacks and sleeping bags, at any given time, other items for sale might have been army sewing kits, axes, wool blankets, feather pillows, wool shirts, men's and women's socks, and rain pants and parkas.

Of course, the store was not high-end retail, so the wool blankets for sale would probably have been in gray or olive drab color, and they might have been used, but cleaned by the government prior to Dad buying them at auction. And the wool shirts would not have been in a fashionable color either, but would probably have been in the standard army color of olive drab. However, if customers could overlook the lack of fashion and color choice, they could get good, sturdy products at good prices at the store.

Now and then, G.I. Joe's, stocked more specialized items, like tank periscopes or windshield defrosters. Of course, they were for sale cheap, because they didn't have standard uses, like, say, wool shirts did. And G.I. Joe's liked to promote its unique bargain merchandise. David told me that store manager, Art Bruer, enjoyed creating signs that said something like, "This cost the government $4,000 and it can be yours for $4.99!"

David said he knew that strategy was successful, because years later, when he was CEO of the business, a lot of folks told him how they had bought certain surplus items from the store's earlier incarnation. They told him how they just hadn't been able to resist buying this or that surplus item, even if they had no idea how to use it, because it had been too good a bargain to pass up!

In thinking of stores today, I would say that Costco comes closest to practicing a retailing strategy like that of G.I. Joe's and

Shopper at checkout counter in Store 1
with clothing department in background, in late 1960s.

other surplus stores of the late 1940s and 1950s. Costco stores seem to constantly vary their product mix and always have items priced lower than standard retail. As a Costco customer, I am motivated to stop by my local store periodically to check on the latest merchandise, just so I don't miss finding some new item I might need or especially want.

It was the same with customers of G.I. Joe's in the 1950s.

Although the flow of army surplus was cut off due to Cold War hostilities in 1960, the range of merchandise for sale at G.I. Joe's actually increased during the next two decades. One reason was because Dad had to find products to sell in place of the surplus. The second reason was that he had a lot more selling space to utilize after Stores 2 and 3 were built next to the original store.

Store 1, after all the additions, covered 56,000 square feet.

Store 2 consisted of 26,000 square feet and Store 3 added another 20,000 square feet. So, the two adjacent stores came close to doubling the selling space of Store 1.

This gave Dad the chance to use great creativity in filling the stores with items to sell. He made the product decisions a little easier by selling different product categories in each store, but there was still quite a range of merchandise in each of them, and some store categories overlapped each other.

He kept shoes, clothing, and housewares merchandise in the first store. In Store 2, he sold outdoor, sporting goods and auto-motive items, making that store a general preview to the G.I. Joe's of the 1990s that had the tagline, "Sports and Automo-tive." Store 3 was the wild card, selling hardware, along with products for customers' hobbies and do-it-yourself projects.

However, even the merchandise in the original Store 1 wasn't always predictable. Although G.I. Joe's did not stock groceries as mentioned before, candy bars were for sale in the first store when I was a kid, and that continued for I don't know how long. And after that store expanded a few times, Dad added popcorn as a treat that customers could buy for 10 cents a bag. Then, sometime in the 1960s, continuing into the early 1970s, Dad added another treat that could be bought at the shoes and clothing/cigarette checkout.

Customers could buy hand-dipped ice cream cones there, choosing from at least a dozen flavors of ice cream, supplied by a local independent, Sunshine Dairy. My brother told me that scooping ice cream for the cones was one of the first jobs of newly-hired cashiers, and it wasn't an easy job. The ice cream often was frozen solid and it could take several scoops to fill a cone because of the difficulty of getting a full scoop.

There was a choice of two sizes. Customers could choose a small cone described as a one-scoop, or a larger, two-scoop one. Allen McMillan, the general contractor in the building of a number of G.I. Joe's stores, suggested to Dad that when someone ordered a cone, the cashier should ask, "Will a large size be OK?"

Dad followed his suggestion and David says that this "subtle upgrade" resulted in a majority of cones being sold in the larger size. I guess you could say G.I. Joe's offered a preview back then of McDonald's policy of asking customers today, if they want to "supersize" their order.

And I must say, I have certainly learned a lot in writing this history. I didn't know that ice cream cones were being sold at the store while I was living in California with my young family, and I surely didn't know that wigs were sold there, too! When David recently said that G.I. Joe's sold wigs in the late 1960s, I was amazed. That is because wigs just didn't seem to fit with the rest of the merchandise being sold at the store, but, in spite of that, my brother said that they sold well.

He said there was a special area for the wigs at the front of the apparel section in Store 1, with four or five cubicles built against the front wall. Inside a cubicle, a customer could sit at a little counter and look in a mirror while trying on wigs of different styles and colors.

Today, wigs seem like they belong only in specialty stores, but they were a general merchandise category in 1969. I can recall receiving a gift of a hair extension that year, which I could use as a ponytail or a fall. Today that would seem like an unusual present, but it didn't seem so then, so I guess wigs and hair extensions were hot items and Dad was just keeping current with a retail trend.

Fabric was another product category added to the first store at about that time. In the mid-1960s, my uncle, Cork Orkney, was retired from selling textiles wholesale and he managed the department. Uncle Cork, known as Roy at the store, also managed the baby furniture area. Yes, for a while, G.I. Joe's sold baby furniture!

David also got involved with selling a type of furniture in Store 1 when G.I. Joe's started selling waterbeds there. It was in the early 1970s, before waterbeds were widely for sale.

David recounted how he took part in a home show at the Portland Expo Center during that time. He would make a sales pitch to passers-by, saying that if they purchased a waterbed, they could be lulled to sleep with the "gentle, wave-like motion" of the bed. Or, they could enjoy the wave-like motion in other ways, too, he would say with a wink.

G.I. Joe's continued to sell waterbeds in their first expansion store in Rockwood in East Multnomah County. The beds were originally featured in the center aisle of the store, and floor drains were installed under the display in case any of the beds sprang a leak.

The second G.I. Joe's store on North Vancouver Avenue featured automotive, sports and outdoor merchandise. Of course, this included everything from motor oil and windshield wipers to tents, hunting rifles, and fishing tackle. Store 2 also sold fishing boats.

The G.I. Joe's surplus store of the 1950s had carried inflatable rafts, but the store of the 1960s and 1970s sold metal dinghies, up to 14 feet in length, along with power motors up to 50 horsepower, according to my brother.

Lawn and garden fertilizers joined the product mix of Store 2 by 1970, followed eventually by plants.

Store 2 shoppers looking at sporting goods in late 1960s. Note tent and fishing poles in background.

A bit of a product overlap occurred between Store 2 and Store 1. The first store sold housewares and cooking items, and the second one stocked cooking items to use outdoors or for cooking customers' fish or game. Cast iron skillets and cookers were big items with hunters and food smokers were especially popular with fishermen.

I couldn't resist the lure of a food smoker when I moved back to the Portland area in 1978. I bought my Little Chief unit along wih wood chips and smoked Tillamook cheddar cheese cubes on my patio. I enjoyed the process and the finished product tasted so good! I can only imagine how satisfying it must have been to customers to smoke fish they had caught themselves.

Store 2 offered many products that continued to be sold in future versions of the business, but that could not be said for Store 3. The last North Portland store sold hobby and do-it-yourself merchandise, along with G.I. Joe's longtime product category of hardware.

David told me that in the late 1960s, Dad was exploring the idea that G.I. Joe's was a "leisure-time" retail business. That, not only should the store offer merchandise for outdoor and sports activities and car repair and upgrading, but it also should stock items used in other leisure pursuits.

That was why you could find rock tumblers and specimen rocks on the shelves of Store 3, along with ceramic supplies, including clay and kilns. Mosaic tile, and molds and resins were for sale, too.

This store also sold fiberglass and foam rubber, both of which were cut to size for customers. David told me that when he was manager of Store 3, this was the department where new employees started out. When new employees were cutting material to a customer's specifications, they were learning to really listen to customers and give them the product just the way they wanted it.

And while Store 1 stocked fabric for sewing, Store 3 stocked fabric for upholstering, both for car and truck seats, and for furniture. The upholstery fabric could be partnered with the foam rubber to make the finished project.

As for hardware, G.I. Joe's had sold it since the first store opened, and it stayed in Store 1 until the third store was built in 1968. Store 3 sold hardware basics, like nuts and bolts and different weights of chains and rope that were both sold by the length. Small hand tools were also featured, and there was a complete plumbing department and electrical department, as well. A full line of indoor and outdoor paint was also offered in this store.

In addition to fabric and cooking utensils, footwear was sold in two of the stores. The original store sold children's, women's, and men's everyday and dress-up shoes, plus men's work boots.

Store 3 shoppers looking at hobby and craft items in late 1960s.
Note sign for ceramic mosaic tile and for craft books.

Included in the work boots line were some with steel toes and even cork boots used in the forest products industry to aid loggers walking on log rafts. David says G.I. Joe's sold a lot of both kinds of boots, and they complemented the men's work clothing for sale in that store.

In the early 1970s, jogging shoes from Blue Ribbon Sports, Phil Knight's shoe company prior to Nike, were sold in the sports-and-auto Store 2. However, David says Chuck Taylor canvas high-tops by Converse were still sold in Store 1.

I guess the only way customers in the late 1960s or early 1970s could have known, with certainty, what was for sale in each of the three stores on North Vancouver Avenue, would have been for them to stop by each one and browse around, as Dad's store slogan used to say.

Ultimately, it was the building of the first expansion store in east Multnomah County that spurred Dad to focus on a more coherent product mix. The footage of the Rockwood Store was only 50,000 square feet, less than half the total footage of the three North Portland stores, which was 112,000 square feet.

It must have been a challenge for Dad to decide which products would be featured in the first branch store and which ones wouldn't. And that was a challenge that, after Dad was gone, David and store management continued to focus on for the duration of the company. ■

Chapter 24

A Brotherhood of
G.I. Surplus Buyers

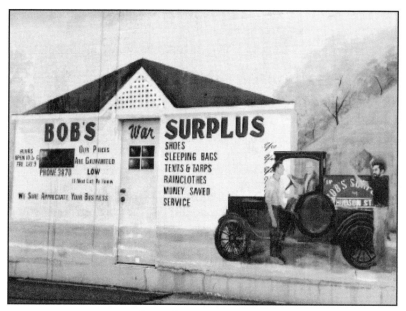

*2013 photo of mural on exterior wall of
Bob's Sporting Goods in Longview, Washington.
It is a tribute to the store's start as Bob's War Surplus.*

W hen I was growing up, part of my father's life was a
mystery to me. Like most children with a parent
who travels for work, I did not really know what
Dad did when he spent time away from home on business. I
knew he attended government auctions at Fort Lewis, McChord
Air Base, or Seattle's Pier 91 in Washington state in order to buy
merchandise to sell, but that was all I knew.

Later he traveled to Seattle to attend monthly meetings of the cooperative buying group, Worldwide Distributors, and these trips were the same kind of mystery to me. What was he doing and who were his associates?

Of course, I didn't think about it much back then. I knew Dad was doing business; that was his job. It is only while writing this book that I have become curious.

I looked at the 50th anniversary newsletter of Worldwide Distributors to learn more about the buying group's history. I discovered that it began when a few army surplus store owners met in the late 1940s while they were buying merchandise at auction at Fort Lewis. According to the newsletter, a group got together in 1951 to place a bid on a large lot that none of them would have been able to bid on individually." These store owners included Bill Jones of Gillingham and Jones of Centralia and later, Chehalis (the business was later named 2 Yard Birds and then shortened to Yard Birds); C. "Tam" Hutchinson of Servicemen's Merchandise in Seattle; W.S. "Bill" Barany of the General Surplus Store in Spokane; F. "Red" Rudisill of the Trading Spot or Best Buy Surplus, also in Spokane; and Bob Schlecht of Bob's Surplus in Longview.

Not long after that initial group got together on an auction bid, these five surplus store owners joined with four more to start meeting regularly as a group.

I learned from talking with Bob Schlecht that the four additional group members were Gene Feldheger of Busy Bee; G.A. "Jerry" Brand of Jerry's Surplus in Everett; George Wakefield of Wakefield's Surplus in Seattle; and George LaMaine of Three G.I.'s in Seattle, as well.

The nine store owners initially met every other week. Their first meeting place was the Hacienda Motel on First Avenue in Seattle, and then they moved the meeting to Tam Hutchinson's warehouse in Seattle's Queen Anne district. In 1954 the nine business owners decided to incorporate and officially start Worldwide Distributors.

Before my Dad joined the buying co-op, all the members' stores were located in Washington state. Then in 1955, Dad with his Oregon store was invited to join Worldwide as the tenth member.

My brother, David, told me that members swapped information about their stores at the monthly meetings. The men had a lot in common since most owned army/navy surplus stores. However, because their stores were in different cities or areas, they were not directly competing with each other. That made it possible for them to be open in their discussions, whether talking about what was selling or comparing advertising strategies.

Charles Grigg of Griggs Department Store in Pasco, Washington, joined Worldwide Distributors in the early 1960s and is still a member today. His three stores in Pasco, Kennewick, and Richland are now affiliated with Ace Hardware as well. We chatted on the phone in the fall of 2013, and he said that the early Worldwide members were a "really great group of guys." Charles said they were all different but shared a love of retail and they all helped each other. What members learned from each other was as valuable as a college education, according to Charles.

It was Charles who suggested that I talk to Bob Schlecht, who, with his wife, Lila, had started Bob's Surplus in Longview, Washington, in the late 1940s. Their much larger store is now called Bob's Sporting Goods and it is still in Longview.

So, I called Bob's Sporting Goods and was delighted to get in touch with him. Bob Schlecht was 92 years old, although with his energy, I would have been unable to guess his age, and only knew it because he shared it with me. He also shared that he had just moved out of his office at the store a few months prior to our conversation.

I had not known any of Dad's friends from Worldwide when I was growing up, and it was moving for me to talk to Bob, who I understand was one of Dad's especially good friends. That my first conversation with Bob took place 37 years after Dad's passing amazed me! I had thought that I knew my dad pretty well, but in researching for this book I discovered so much more about him.

Bob told me stories about my father, including one about a fishing trip that Dad and David took with Bob and his son, Bobby. Evidently Dad and David were sleeping away in a tent while Bobby caught a 47-pound fish! David told me later that Dad caught a big fish on that trip, too, although not a 47-pounder.

Bob Schlecht said he had believed in the power of advertising early on, because his store got results from it, but Dad would not advertise back then. Bob relayed how he had tried so hard to get Dad to advertise a sale of a large auction lot of life preservers, but Dad would have none of it.

Bob urging Dad to advertise is an example of how Worldwide members gave advice to each other and tried to help everyone grow their business. Bob said the biggest challenge a member of the buying group had was to figure out how to help other members.

For instance, a practice Dad learned from another member was to carry a magnet when he was previewing government auctions. That was because most metal items were painted either the army olive-drab color or the navy gray, disguising what kind of metal it was made of. With the help of a magnet, Dad would find the items made out of steel, because, of course, the magnet stuck to them. If the magnet didn't stick, the item might be made out of brass.

Knowing that, Dad could buy it to sell as metal scrap if he thought the item wouldn't sell well in the store. Brass sold for a lot more than steel back then, and does today, too. I found in my research that scrap items made of brass currently sell for about ten times the price of steel items.

Two of Dad's friends in Worldwide Distributors were Jim Anderson and Ed Baxter of the Andy and Bax Store in Portland. David told the story of how he once accompanied Dad to Andy and Bax in order to pick up a pallet of surplus. Instead of Dad paying Jim and Ed directly for the merchandise, the three men decided to wager it in a poker game. And one of them pulled out a whiskey bottle to make the game more enjoyable!

I understand that poker games were also played at Worldwide gatherings, at least some of the time. One game played was Liars Poker, using the serial numbers on dollar bills to make poker hands. That was the same game Dad liked to play when I would visit him from Southern California in the 1970s, and we would go out with other store folks to eat lunch at Waddles Restaurant at Jantzen Beach.

Incidentally, my Aunt Joey (Jo) Stout Hadfield, who owned G.I. Stores in Salem in the 1960s and 1970s, became the first female member of Worldwide in 1966, I believe. Aunt Joey remembers that there were about 20 members in the co-op at that time.

Worldwide Distributors continues on today, still headquartered in the Seattle area, but now in Kent instead of the city center. And Dad is still linked with present-day Worldwide because he and David found the property in Kent where the co-op is still located, according to Bob Schlecht. Bob also stated that Dad and David negotiated the purchase of the property for Worldwide, too.

The Worldwide Distributors' website describes the group as a member-owned, member-directed cooperative that started in 1955 and now has 50 employees and access to more than 3,000 vendors. What a good buying group for independent retailers!

Looking back to the beginning of the group, an article in the 50th anniversary edition of the Worldwide newsletter had these insights: "We note that many of the early participants were veterans that experienced a world war that required peoples of all types to band together to succeed. We cannot help but wonder if that experience influenced their ease with building trusting relationships with other retailers and freely giving all they could to help the other guy." ■

Chapter 25

G.I. Joe's and Other Northwest Surplus Stores

*Sad Sack character at side entrance of Store No. 1 in
North Portland in 1964, drawing attention to signs listing items for sale.*

The start-up and early growth of G.I. Joe's was compara-
ble to the beginnings of many surplus stores in the
Pacific Northwest. That is what I discovered looking
through material supplied to me by Mark Williams, President of
Worldwide Distributors in 2013.

The 2005 newsletter of Worldwide Distributors that celebrated 50 years of being in business profiled six of the early member stores, five of which started business as surplus stores. These five stores included Bob's Surplus in Longview; the Army/Navy Store and Big Ray's in Alaska; Swain's General Store in Port Angeles; Tri-State Distributors in Moscow, Idaho; and G.I. Joe's in Portland. The other member store profiled was Grigg's Department Store in Pasco, Washington, which began as a hardware and appliance store.

As I read the store histories, I saw similarities in the beginnings of these businesses and G.I. Joe's, including what some of the owners did prior to opening stores. For instance, Dad initially sold merchandise out of his vehicle, mostly in Oregon. So did Lee Connelly of Tri-State Distributors. Lee traveled through three states selling army surplus, according to the newsletter.

Early Worldwide members were flexible in their choice of retail outlets. In 1946, George LaMaine and his two partners in the 3 G.I.'s store in Seattle started selling war surplus in former military tents. As mentioned earlier, Dad also sold merchandise in tents in three different Portland stores from 1948 to 1952, and in 1956, Cliff Swain of the Swain's General Store of Port Angeles started his store in a tent, too.

The newsletter said Bob's Surplus in Longview started in a small building in 1947, and that the owner, Bob Schlecht, shared space in the building on Saturdays with local women selling fruit and vegetables. And Rich Gillingham and Bill Jones, owners of Yard Birds in Chehalis, housed some of their retail business in army surplus Quonset huts.

I guess the bottom line for these entrepreneurs was that they had merchandise to sell and they didn't need a fancy place to do it in. And the merchandise didn't have a phased delivery schedule if you bought it at auction. "You bought it, you got it!" So, they had to move it right away to keep their overhead down, which led Dad and others to be creative with their selling space.

The surplus store owners weren't necessarily attached to selling in one location, either. Dad is an example, starting his first store in Salem before opening one in Portland. Yard Birds' owners, Bill Jones and Rich Gillingham, started their first store in Centralia, Washington, before they moved to Chehalis.

Also, according to the Worldwide newsletter, business partners Glen Miller and Howard Cruver were in Seattle in 1948, when they decided that Alaska would be a great place to sell army surplus. Shortly thereafter, they opened a store in Anchorage. In 2005, the business still had two retail operations in that state, Army/Navy Store and Big Ray's, the Worldwide newsletter reported.

The members of the buying group often had unusual names for their stores. Of course, there was G.I. Joe's, which took a nickname for servicemen in World War II as the store name. There was also the 2 Yard Birds store in Centralia and that evolved into the Yard Birds store in Chehalis. Yardbirds was a nickname for servicemen who hung around military supply yards.

Other unique store names for early members of the buying co-op included Busy Bee, Three G.I.'s, and Chubby and Tubby, which had two stores in the Seattle area. And Gene Feldheger's Buck Private Store appeared on a member's list in 1961. Not as unusual, but still uniquely named, were Big Ray's in Alaska and Andy and Bax in Portland.

Sometimes, Worldwide members used similar mascot or I.D. characters for their businesses. Yard Birds, with their 1947 start-up store Centralia, used two "Sad Sack-like" characters in their signage. Sad Sack was a popular cartoon character of an army private created during World War II by George Baker. Yard Birds did take-offs on the character and created "Skinny" and "Fatty" to represent owners Rich Gillingham and Bill Jones.

Dad followed them and also used a character similar to Sad Sack, at least in 1964, as shown in the photo of the first store in North Portland. I was living in Portland at the time but just don't recall the image or know when Dad stopped using it.

Yard Birds at some point also stopped using the "Skinny and Fatty" characters and instead, developed a memorable cartoon bird character that looked like a smiling crow to use as the symbol of the store.

In 1971, according to the history timeline on Yard Birds' website, the business went far beyond depicting their logo character in print, and constructed a 60-foot tall sculpture of the bird! The figure was made out of a metal rebar frame covered with fiberglass and then painted. The huge bird was situated at the entrance to the Yard Birds store and could be seen from the nearby I-5 Freeway.

Customers could even drive their cars through the bird's legs! Unfortunately, that access led to the demise of the giant bird, which burned up in 1976 after a customer's car caught fire while under it and the car fire ignited the fiberglass bird.

The bird motif was also used by Lee Hobbs in Medford, Oregon, when he opened a surplus store in 1965 and named it the Black Bird Store. The Black Bird Shopping Center website in 2013 said that Lee built a 29-foot tall black bird for the business, fashioning it "after a 10-foot magpie at a store called Yard Birds up in Centralia, Washington, owned by a friend of Lee's."

The use of similar mascots or logo characters at different stores demonstrates in a really graphic way the sharing that occurred between members of Worldwide Distributors.

Members all faced similar challenges. Belonging to Worldwide solved the first, most basic dilemma of keeping the wholesale cost of merchandise low enough so that these smaller stores could compete with larger ones.

The changing world situation brought the next major challenge in 1960 when the government stopped surplus auctions because of the threat of possible military action with the Soviet Union when that country built the Berlin Wall, dividing East and West Berlin.

The owners had to deal with the major question of what to sell instead of government-issued merchandise. Worldwide was able to line up vendors for members that might not have been available to store owners individually.

The members faced another major challenge years later, when national chains with big box stores began moving into areas previously dominated by local stores. This was huge! National retailers started moving into the Northwest in the 1970s and the trend continues today as chains like Wal-Mart keep looking for additional expansion locations.

Of course, this wasn't the first time, at least for some of the Worldwide members, that they had faced the possibility of daunting competition. In the 1950s and 1960s, before big box stores, there was the competition in Portland from Fred Meyer. Very popular "Freddie's" sold groceries, variety, pharmacy items, clothing, and gardening merchandise, using their "one-stop shopping" format in large store locations.

I guess during those early years there was enough distance between the North Portland G.I. Joe's and Fred Meyer stores, so that there was not direct competition. And when that competition happened with the building of the first expansion store in Rockwood in 1970, Dad was very pleased that G.I. Joe's was still able to thrive.

Store survival was never a given for any of the member stores of Worldwide Distributors. However, many managed to stay in business, often opting to remain in one location and expand there, sometimes many times. One store that followed that model was Yard Birds, which was the dominant member of Worldwide, with Bill Jones serving as President of the group for many years. The Yard Birds store grew to 110,000 square feet in 1958. According to the timeline on the store's history website, it had 16 departments and five businesses renting space in the store at that time.

Topping that, in 1971, Rich Gillingham and Bill Jones opened their huge new Yard Birds store of 305,000 square feet, with 350 employees! Their history website says the store sold general merchandise, and also featured a restaurant, cocktail lounge, a car wash; plus, it leased space to a grocery store, and a bank.

G.I. Joe's followed the path of expanding in place through the 1960s, but in the 1970s, Dad decided to go in a different direction and started adding locations around Portland. Some of the other Worldwide members also added branch stores, for instance, Yard Birds opened the Sea Mart store in Olympia in 1959. However, I don't believe other stores' expansions were done with the same standardized approach that Dad and David employed when they started opening branch locations in Portland and beyond.

Luck seems to have played a large part in the growth of G.I. Joe's because of its prime retail location and because it was in Portland. In the 1970s, this city, built on the confluence of the Willamette and Columbia Rivers, was an ideal size for a store to add branch stores that were somewhat close to each other, making it easy to distribute merchandise.

Portland was also an ideal size for building customer awareness throughout the area with advertising (when Dad finally started advertising.) Portland was one basic media market, with two and then one major newspaper, radio stations serving the whole city, and, only a few TV stations prior to cable TV.

On the other hand, knowing Dad, perhaps the placement of G.I. Joe's wasn't due to luck after all. I know that he first capitalized on the unique store location near Vancouver, Washington, which drew customers looking to avoid Washington State sales tax and cigarette tax. Maybe he also took into consideration the special characteristics of Portland when he opened his first G.I. Joe's and when he chose to begin expanding.

At any rate, the store kept adding branches, first in Oregon and then in Washington. As Mark Williams of Worldwide wrote me in July, 2013, "With the closure of Yard Birds, and later, the exit of Academy Sports based in Texas, G.I. Joe's was to become the predominate member of the group (Worldwide) at the beginning of the new century."

Mark went on to say that "G.I. Joe's had the vision to imitate big box retailers." And in 2008, which was the last full year of operation for the business, the company (by that time, Joe's Sports, Outdoor and More) purchased over $35 million in goods through Worldwide.

Looking back at the early years, I know Worldwide Distributors certainly contributed to Dad's and the store's success in at least three major ways. First, it gave his small store, and later small chain, the ability to place orders with major, brand-name suppliers. The second benefit Worldwide offered G.I. Joe's was the ability to pool the store's orders with other members' orders to get a reduction in the wholesale cost of merchandise. A third benefit for Dad was a chance to gain knowledge from the open sharing of information among early members.

And on a personal level, I think a benefit beyond measure for Dad and other members was the development of solid and enduring friendships with each other.

Not bad, for an organization that began as an informal group of guys meeting together at government auctions near Seattle in the late 1940s and early 1950s! They played a little poker, decided to do some group bids on auction lots, and eventually formed a buying cooperative that is still going strong. ■

Chapter 26

Dad's Story

*Dad holding David in Salem in 1947, the year
Dad's first surplus store opened.*

M y father opened his first war surplus store when I was three years old, so he had a store almost as far back as I can remember. As a kid, that was just the way it was, but I now realize that Dad could have taken many different vocational paths after he was discharged from the Army Air Forces in 1945.

He could have looked for a job right away, or he could have attended college on the G.I. Bill as so many veterans did. With a college degree, good jobs would have been available to him. But Dad did not want to work for someone else. He had a dream of starting his own business, and a loan from his mother made that possible.

As previously related, he bought some G.I. sleeping bags at auction with the loan, and that set him on the path of buying surplus and selling it wholesale to stores or retail to customers at various outdoor locations. Between 1947 and 1951, Dad was involved with the start-up of three war surplus stores, none of which lasted, but he kept going. He never gave up, even when he briefly worked in a plywood mill on the Willamette River during this time.

Finally, in 1952, Dad got the business right when he bought a small surplus store in a G.I. hospital tent in North Portland called G.I. Joe's.

For Dad to be involved in the opening of four stores in five years took ambition, self-confidence and a lot of hard work. However, his vision of starting a successful business must have wavered occasionally. My Aunt Joey once reminisced about a time when she was a dinner guest at our North Portland home, around 1949. After dinner, my father lay down on the floor to relax, looked up at Mom and asked, "Do you think we are ever going to amount to anything?"

Studying my grandparents helps me to understand Dad better. His father, Roydon, was a businessman who was willing to take risks, and his mother, Mary, was creative. She was an artist who studied painting in San Francisco and Paris. Mary and Roydon met in San Jose, California, and married in nearby Campbell in 1900. I believe the families had farms there, possibly growing plums, and I heard a family story that Roydon also sold water from an artesian well on his family's property.

*Dad standing in front of his five brothers and parents,
Mary and Roydon, in Hoquiam, circa 1917.*

In 1907, my grandparents left the security of San Jose to move to the boomtown of Lloydminster, Saskatchewan, Canada. My grandfather had been born in Quebec City, Quebec, and spent his early years there, so moving to Canada may have felt like going home to him. He started a mercantile store in Lloydminster. Then he and Mary packed their three sons into a wagon and traveled across the Canadian prairie to Edmonton, Alberta. There, my grandfather opened another dry goods store. He went on to open two more stores, one in the growing town of Edson, Alberta, and another in Prince Rupert, British Columbia.

Dad helps his mother, Mary in her "war garden," in 1917.

I learned of my grandparents' travels from writings of my uncle, Sydney Orkney, which were given to me by my cousin, Mary Lynn Conlon. What my uncle didn't say was how long the stores stayed in business or when they were closed. But apparently, opening four stores in small but growing towns in Canada was not enough of a challenge for my grandfather! At some point, Roydon and a business friend decided to seek their fortunes prospecting for gold in Alaska, leaving Mary in charge of whatever stores remained, while he was gone.

The two friends did not find gold. When Roydon returned, he sold the remaining store in Edmonton, Alberta, and the fam-

Dad, on the right, sits on steps with his older brother, Donald, in Hoquiam, 1919.

ily moved to Hoquiam, Washington. The twin cities of Hoquiam and Aberdeen on Grays Harbor were booming because of the logging in the area, and my grandfather opened yet another general store.

Dad was born in Hoquiam in 1915, and was welcomed into the family by five older brothers. They were, from oldest to youngest, Woolston (known as Cork), James, Sydney, Douglas, and Donald. Shortly before Dad turned 14 in 1929, the stock market crashed and the Great Depression descended on his family, causing great financial hardship, as it did for so many American families.

Mom and Dad in Hoquiam, circa 1941.

One consequence of the Depression was that it kept my dad from earning a college degree. Although at least two of his older brothers graduated from the University of Washington, there was no money left in the family to pay for Dad's college tuition when he graduated from high school in 1933. But he still managed to attend the University of Washington for one year, according to records I've found, while working full-time, including at a bakery and waiting tables at a fraternity.

I don't know what Dad's experiences were as a freshman at the University of Washington, but there must have been some unpleasantness. What I do know is that his time at college left him with an aversion for exclusive organizations and pretentious people, and he even came to doubt the worth of a college education.

The next few years were hard for him financially, and he moved from job to job around the country. At one point, he drove cars from Detroit to the West Coast and spent some time chauffeuring in Los Angeles. My brother says Dad also worked as a union organizer in Detroit for a short time, organizing grocery store clerks in that time before supermarkets.

Dad eventually returned to take business classes in Hoquiam, where he met Charmian Munson in 1938 or 1939. They were married in 1942, the same year Dad was inducted into the army and started officers' training and flight school in the Army Air Corps.

After returning to civilian life in 1945, Dad must have looked at the work paths of his parents and older brothers, trying to decide how to support his young family. In addition to his father, Roydon, who had started at least five general stores in various cities in western Canada and in Hoquiam, his mother had also opened a dress shop in the Hoquiam area.

By 1945, Dad's brothers James and Sydney had become successful businessmen. Jim and Syd lived in Yakima, Washington, and worked as partners in an insurance brokerage firm that Jim had started with another partner in 1937. After the war, Jim also opened a real estate agency and briefly owned a sand and gravel company. But Jim's largest venture was growing hops, which he began farming in the early 1940s. At one time, Jim was the largest independent hop grower in the Yakima Valley according to his son Bruce. And this was when Yakima was the largest hops-growing region in the country.

Looking at the other three brothers, Cork was a salesman in

Roydon Orkney sits with his 4 surviving sons.
From left to right are Sydney, Cork, Roydon, Dad, and James
in Portland in 1959.

Los Angeles, and Dad's two other brothers died young. Douglas died in an auto accident in California in 1938, and Donald was killed in a glider crash in 1945, while serving in the Army Air Forces in the Philippines during World War II.

So when Dad was ready to start a career after his discharge from the Army Air Forces in 1945, only Cork (in Dad's immediate family) was working for someone else. Dad did not choose to follow Cork's example. Instead, he followed his parents and other two brothers and started his own business. And he chose to go into retail, as his parents had done. ■

Chapter 27

Mom's Story

Mom (left) sits with her brother Miles and sister Joey, in 1929.

My mother, Charmian Munson, was born in El Dorado, Kansas, a small town in America's heartland, to Anne Marie Doores Munson and Mahlon Standish Munson. Mom was the middle child between her older brother, Miles, and younger sister, Georgia Ann, who most often went by the name, Joey.

Mom's parents both came from small Midwest towns. Marie had grown up on a farm outside the small town of Bronaugh, Missouri, while Mahlon had grown up in town, in El Dorado, Kansas, the eventual birthplace of Mom, as well. I believe that Marie's family thought of themselves as Southerners and they

Mahlon was a cadet at The Citadel.
His hat sits on top of a pyramid of cannon balls in this undated photo.

attended the Bronaugh Methodist-Episcopal Church South that her father helped to build. Mahlon's family, on the other hand, identified with the Union side in the Civil War and his father served in the Union Army.

It is interesting that Mahlon did attend The Citadel Military College in Charleston, South Carolina, but I recall a family story that he attended school there, not because it was in the South, but because he wanted to prepare to enlist in the armed services in World War I. However, after attending the military school, serving in the armed forces overseas was not to be for my grandfather. He tried to enlist and was rejected by every branch of service because bouts of childhood pneumonia had adversely affected his lungs.

The family story of Marie and Mahlon's courtship was that it was

Marie shows off her target shooting skills.

love at first sight. Marie was visiting her sister in El Dorado when Mahlon met her in front of a shop. After that one meeting, he told the friend he was with that he was going to marry Marie! Perhaps the family differences were somewhat challenging, though, because Marie and Mahlon traveled across the state line to Oklahoma to get married in 1917. That was a daring move, but their many loving years together proved that Mahlon made a wise choice when he decided he was going to marry Marie the first time he met her.

Just like Dad's family, Mom's family was adventurous, and Marie and Mahlon drove 1,800 miles of rough and often dirt roads from Kansas to California in a Model T Ford. I am not sure when they made that trip, but it must have been shortly after the wedding. In California, Mahlon attended Stanford University in Palo Alto for a while, and worked at Dudfield Lumber Company. Then he and Marie moved on when he got a job as mill manager at the Campbell-Redwood Lumber Company

Marie had been a tomboy when she was growing up on the farm, horseback riding and target shooting with her three brothers and two sisters. That tomboy spirit prevailed at the lumber mill where my 18-year-old, future grandmother dashed across a floating log boom. I guess she didn't stop to think that she could have fallen between the logs and drowned, but my grandfather certainly must have thought of that when he heard about my grandmother's adventure.

I can sympathize with that young woman who became my grandmother; growing up is hard to do! It must have been especially difficult for a young woman living in a lumber camp near the lumber mill, far from home and family, in the early decades of the twentieth century, when expectations of women's correct behavior were so much more limited and confining than expectations today.

Just a few weeks after starting work at the lumber mill, Mahlon was drafted into the army for stateside duty. The couple moved to Tacoma, Washington, and my grandfather served at Camp Lewis, until his discharge in early 1919.

By the time their first child, Miles, was born in 1920, Marie and Mahlon were back in California, living in Oakland. Then, when Miles was about a year old, the family packed up and moved back to Kansas because they had heard of possible opportunities there because of the oil boom.

Mother was born in El Dorado in 1921. A job opportunity related to the oil discoveries near there did not materialize for Mahlon, so in 1922, the family moved to Kansas City and settled down. In Kansas City, my grandfather continued working in the

*Marie and baby Miles at Donner Lake, during the family's
10-day trip back to Kansas from California.*

lumber business, but in marketing and advertising, and Marie took
care of the family, including my Aunt Joey, who was born in 1926.

The 1929 stock market crash changed everything for them.
Mahlon lost his job, and the family leased out their home and
moved to San Antonio, Texas, where my grandfather worked as
Executive Director of the Lumber Research Bureau. That job lasted
only a year. Then, with no money coming in, my mom's family lost
their home and all its contents, and they returned to El Dorado to
live with Mahlon's mother, Genevieve Mather Munson. My grandfather ran the family movie theater and started a soda fountain.

In researching about my mother during those hard times, I heard that she had a lot of energy and a robust sense of humor. And I can see from photos of Mom as a child that she was pretty. Like a lot of little girls, she took dancing lessons and performed in recitals.

Her special sparkle impressed Mahlon's brother, Arthur, who worked for a Hollywood studio in the lighting department. When Mom was about 11 years old and Uncle Arthur and family were visiting El Dorado, he suggested to Marie and Mahlon that they bring

Mom poses in her dance recital costume in Kansas City, in May 1929.

Charmian to Hollywood, and he would see to it that she got a screen test.

I could really see my mother as a movie star, but that was not in her future. My grandparents said, "Absolutely not!" No child of theirs was going to be in the movies!

From El Dorado, Mom's family moved to Detroit, Michigan, where her dad worked for yet another company until it went bankrupt. Then it was on to the Pacific Northwest and another job opportunity that beckoned him.

Mahlon did find a job at the Douglas Fir Plywood Association

Mom at Alamo in San Antonio, Texas, in 1942, where Dad took pilot training.

in Tacoma, and the family first lived on Vashon Island near Seattle, and then in Tacoma, where my mother graduated from Stadium High School in 1937. That summer, the family moved again, this time, south to Hoquiam where my grandfather worked in advertising and marketing for a plywood mill.

Mom told me that she attended the College of Puget Sound, (now University of Puget Sound) freshman year. Then, she returned to Hoquiam and enrolled in business school, probably in 1938. When she left business school in 1940, Mom got a job as a private secretary and saved her money to buy a car.

She bought a shiny new Packard Coupe, according to my aunt, and proudly drove it off the display floor. Two blocks later, she was so excited to be behind the wheel of her new car, that she rear-ended the car in front of her.

Mom must have been momentarily distracted from the road, and, because of it, she got to enjoy her new Packard Coupe for only two blocks before it had to go into the shop!

Looking back, I can see clearly how talented my mother was.

I believe she could have succeeded in many different roles, had she chosen to do so. But she chose to be content performing on the family stage for her parents and siblings and then for the family she and Dad created, with me, David, and the store. In many ways, I think the family stage was not big enough for her with all her talents, and I wonder what she would have contributed to the world at large, if she had lived in a later time when it was more usual for a woman to have a career.

But American public sentiment in the late 1940s and 1950s was that women belonged in the home. Just look at print advertisements of the time! That was just the way things were, after the troops came back from World War II and needed jobs.

So, my mother used her abundant energy to make sure that our home always shone, that delicious dinners were hot on the table, and that she looked like a dream in the clothes she made. Mom also made most of my clothes until I was in the fourth grade. I got compliments on my dresses (we did not wear jeans to school in those days), and my standard answer was, "Thank you. My mother made it."

Outside, at our home on Columbia Avenue in the early 1950s, Mom planted laurel bushes on two sides of the yard, and they grew into a hedge, over time. The first few summers after planting, David and I would take the hose from bush to bush every few days, watering the plants. That was just one of our summer chores.

Mom also conducted a personal vendetta against lupine plants that would pop up in the spring between the driveway and the Flo-Bob Kennel next door. Today, I enjoy the lupine's conical, purple bloom, but Mom didn't share my taste in the 1950s! I think she was trying to civilize our yard by planting the laurel bushes or vining sweet peas in the spring. Lupines were

Mom holds her poodle, Jacques in Portland in 1960.

wild and grew on their own, instead of being planted.

Around 1954, Mom decided she wanted more storage, so she built some drawers and a cupboard in an unfinished room off the dining room. I had a memory of her sawing a piece of wood on sawhorses, but I wasn't sure I was remembering correctly until I checked with Aunt Joey. My aunt assured me that Mom did build the drawers and cupboard. Where did she learn her carpentry skills? I don't know!

She delighted in giving us nicknames. My brother David inherited the Orkney nickname, Corky, and that was what we mostly called him. She named me Tootie and gave Dad the name, Dude. That name did not set well with my Uncle Cork. He complained in later years that we should not call my father Dude, but Rock, because he was such a rock and support to the extended family.

However, Mom's nickname prevailed, and Dad was called Dude for the rest of his life by the three of us. However, I never heard anyone outside the family use the name. Dad was known as Ed or Edward to everyone else.

Mom even gave a name to the unfinished room where she built the drawers and cupboard. She named it Corregidor, after Corregidor Island at the entrance to Manila Bay in the Philippines, which was made famous during World War II. General Douglas MacArthur escaped from this island in 1942 as Japanese forces were taking over the Philippines. After MacArthur's harrowing journey to Australia, he made his famous vow, "I shall return." In 1944, MacArthur and American troops did return to the Philippines, and in 1945 the country was liberated after the final surrender of Japan to the Allied Forces.

I don't know why Mom chose that name; maybe it was because she was so motivated to improve the house, and yet it felt like a big deal for her to build the storage herself, so she was comparing her project to General MacArthur leaving the island in Manila Bay. Or, maybe I'm infusing way too much drama into the name! It could have been Mom's way of noting that the room was not a part of the main house, just as like Corregidor was not part of the mainland. But whatever Mom had in mind, the nickname demonstrates how World War II continued to cast its shadow over my family.

Mom gave our family so much, from delicious meals and a spotless, well-decorated home to hand-sewn dresses for me, but I think I'm most grateful that she surrounded us with laughter. She always looked for the humor in a situation and tried to make even mundane things fun for us. This included family gatherings where she and her sister, Joey, got together, and their laughter was nonstop. The laughter was contagious and we all joined in. ■

Chapter 28

Mom and Dad Together

Just married! February 1942, in Port Townsend, Washington

As you can gather from earlier chapters, Mom and her family moved around a lot when she was young, and Dad moved around a lot after his one year at the University of Washington in 1933 and 1934. However, my future mom and dad both wound up living in Hoquiam, attending a local business school. That is where they met, probably in 1938, when Mom returned to live with her family after her freshman year at College of Puget Sound in Tacoma.

They began dating, and a year or two later, Dad asked Mom to marry him in a very unusual way, according to my Aunt

Joey. Flying in a small plane over the house where Mom lived with her family in Hoquiam, Dad leaned out of the open cockpit and tried to drop a fake engagement ring down to her that he had tied to a small, handmade parachute! However, the wind carried away the parachute and ring, neither of which were ever found. Thank goodness the ring was not the real thing.

Dad had even arranged for a newspaper reporter to be there to record the ring drop. What amazes me about this story is that the Dad I knew was quite modest and not a person who made dramatic gestures. I would never have imagined him trying to propose with an engagement ring dropped from an airplane! He must have loved Mom very much to ask for her hand in marriage in such a big and romantic way, knowing that she would love it.

In the bigger picture, war was on the horizon, with fighting consuming much of Europe and some of Asia. Dad joined the Army Reserves in September 1940. When the U.S. entered the war after the Japanese bombed Pearl Harbor on December 7, 1941, Dad's service status changed to active duty.

Exactly two months after the bombing of Pearl Harbor, my parents were married in Port Townsend, Washington. As you can see from the photo, Dad was wearing his uniform. Mom, who forgot to pack her wedding veil, is wearing an impromptu one made from tulle her mother bought from a local store just before the ceremony.

As related before, Dad transferred from a Coast Artillery unit to the Army Air Forces after passing the test for officer's training. He was assigned to various air bases for flight training, including bases in Arizona and Texas, and my mother accompanied him. In April, 1943, he graduated from the Air Force Advanced Flying

Envelope and letter dad sent to his mother from New Guinea in 1944, while serving as a bomber pilot in the Army Air Forces.

School of Altus, Oklahoma and shipped out to New Guinea later in the summer. And as noted earlier, he was assigned to the 90th Bomb Group or the Jolly Rogers, assigned to the Fifth Air Force.

Mom was pregnant with me by then, and she returned to Hoquiam to live with her parents. Of course Mom and Dad wrote letters to each other, but it took a long time for letters to be delivered because of the war. And being wartime, an army censor would have read Dad's letter before Mom received it. This is evident from an envelope and letter of Dad's that I have, which had been sent to his mother. I can see where the censor's tape closed up the side of the envelope that is now yellowed, and writing on the tape noted that the letter was "Opened by U.S. Army Examiner." On the back of the envelope was stamped the Jolly Rogers bomb group logo.

In early 1944 I was born while Dad was still overseas.

Dad met me for the first time when he returned home in August 1944 and was reunited with Mom. He remained in the Army Air Forces and the three of us moved to Riverside, California, in 1945 when he was assigned to duty there. After Dad's service discharge, we returned to the Pacific Northwest.

In 1946, we were back in Hoquiam and that was where my brother, David, was born. By the time he was a year old, we were living in Salem, Oregon, where Dad opened his first army surplus store with a business partner he knew from the Army Air Forces.

While writing this story, I was struck to see how much World War II impacted our family life. It surprised me because I never thought about it growing up. Now I can see that it affected us quite a bit.

I have to look no further than the work my father was doing and the store he started. He didn't open just any retail business, but an army surplus business, selling merchandise left over from the war. For the business name, Dad used G.I. Joe's, a nickname for servicemen during World War II. And he associated for the rest of his life with many veterans in the merchandise buying group to which he belonged.

The other world situation that had a strong influence on Dad and Mom was the Great Depression. Both of their families had been severely impacted by it, and it had given my parents a strong desire for financial security. They were both very careful with money and taught my brother and me to be careful, too. Doing an honest day's work, paying your bills, and having good credit were important to them, and we learned that from them.

Their goal was not to be wealthy, but to be secure, to have enough so they would not ever again experience the kind of hardship they did in the 1930s and early 1940s. Today, it seems like everyone wants to be rich, but my parents didn't think that way, and I don't believe many of their contemporaries did either.

In thinking about my parents together, I have to say that Mom was the outgoing one. She was intelligent and witty, with a great sense of humor. She was creative, too, demonstrated by her sewing and knitting when I was young. An afghan she knit when I was young even won an award at the Oregon State Fair.

One of Mom's qualities that really stood out for me was her positive outlook on life. I don't know if it came naturally or had been nurtured by her upbringing as a Christian Scientist. The grace we used to say at dinner sums it up: "For those leaning on the sustaining Infinite, today is big with blessings."

The other outstanding quality I remember was her strong will-power. If Mom wanted to get something done, you could bet that she would. And combining that with her positive mental outlook meant that it would be done with a smile!

Dad also possessed a positive life view and a strong will. But in contrast to Mom, Dad was quiet and focused on what he was doing.

Mom and Dad worked well together in many ways. You could look at Dad as the sole creator of G.I. Joe's, but I think the store was a product of their partnership. Dad brought the store into reality, and Mom supplied the backup.

And yet, that was not enough to keep them together. My parents separated in 1963, 11 years after Dad's G.I. Joe's store first opened its doors in North Portland. David was a senior at Madison High School, and I was attending Portland State

Dad with Mom holding Jamil at Christmas in 1966.

College at the time. It seems to me that Mom and Dad got back together for a while, but then split again in 1964. That was when David was attending the University of Oregon and I had moved out of the family home to live closer to Portland State, where I was still going to school.

I believe Mom and Dad divorced sometime in 1965 or 1966. They both eventually remarried; Mom married Edward Halligan, and Dad married Arlene Bissonette.

However, even after their divorce and remarriages, which I believe were happy, it was obvious that my parents continued to love and respect each other until Dad's death in 1976. ■

Chapter 29

Dad's Strengths

*Dad receiving 1973 national Buyers Award from the
Associated Surplus Dealers (ASD) at their trade show in Las Vegas.
This may have been the only award or honor Dad ever received for G.I. Joe's.*

I believe a spirit of competition existed between Dad and two of his older brothers and that helped motivate him to start his own business, just like they had done. But it took more than a competitive spirit for him to build a thriving retail chain from scratch. What other strengths or gifts did he possess that helped him be successful?

The first gift I would point to was his brain power. Dad was very intelligent, and he told me that he had been a voracious reader while growing up. Once, he became so immersed in reading *The Adventures of Robin Hood* that he ran out of the house and into the street, shouting, "Prince John is coming; Prince John is coming!"

175

My cousin Bruce Orkney, son of my uncle Jim, said that on one of his visits to the old Orkney household, our grandmother told him how much Dad enjoyed reading. She pointed to a particular chair where Dad would sit, always engrossed in a book. Bruce added, "She said he would have a big dictionary next to him and looked up every word he didn't know."

Bruce fondly remembers visiting his father's family when some, or all, of his father's five brothers were present in the Hoquiam family home, in the mid to late 1930s. "It was always fascinating for me to be around these Orkneys," Bruce said. "They seemed to always be involved in heated discussions about most everything, including world affairs, the economy, business, and especially politics. The conversations were fun and always spirited."

This tradition of heated family discussions must have helped Dad in later years when he needed to analyze business situations and trends. Also, his constant reading showed a desire for knowledge.

Dad also had leadership qualities. Obviously, becoming an officer in the Army Air Forces helped develop his potential as a leader. And as mentioned previously, Bruce remembers that he was promoted to squadron leader and then group squadron leader in his B-24 bomb group in New Guinea in 1943 and 1944.

My brother and I didn't learn that information from my father because another one of his most entrenched qualities was modesty. Bragging was not something he did. A simple statement of the facts was OK, but drawing attention yourself was not.

Dad wouldn't even celebrate his birthday! He didn't want us to mention it or give him presents or a birthday cake. He claimed it was because his family had a religious background as Quakers, but he gave no evidence for that claim. In fact, I recently found out from a genealogy website that his father had been confirmed in the Episcopal Church in San Jose, California, as a young man, so I don't know what background he was referring to. Dad's desire not to have a birthday celebration might have been just because just he didn't want to be the center of attention, not because of any religious beliefs.

SLEEPING BAGS
Lowest Prices In Town!
G. I. JOE'S
8700 N. Vancouver Ave.

Small ad that ran in The Oregonian *classified section in 1952 and 1953.*

Dad's personal modesty and basic quietness were reflected in the store's advertising policy. In 1952, I assume after Dad bought G.I. Joe's, I found only two, large classified ads in *The Oregonian* that ran in March. They were for canvas tarpaulins, priced by weight and per square foot. The advertisement said the tarps were waterproofed, mildew resistant, with grommets and double stitched seams. They were 8 cents per square foot for light weight, 9.5 cents per square foot for medium weight, and 11 cents per square foot for heavy weight.

The ad also mentioned tents, "set up and displayed. See and know what you're buying."

This ad, which ran twice, is the only large ad, either classified or display that I could find from G.I. Joe's in the early years of Dad's ownership. It is interesting, to me, that there was no heavy promotion, just a statement of fact about what was for sale. And the idea of full disclosure for the tents was emphasized, so that a customer would know just what product they were buying.

There was an advertisement that did run in *The Oregonian* classifieds and sometimes in the sports section during 1952 and

1953. It was one small ad, a column wide and probably an inch high. It simply said, "Sleeping Bags, Lowest Prices in Town! G.I. JOE'S, 8700 N. Vancouver Ave." Again, it was a basic ad, although it did make the claim of "Lowest Prices in Town!"

That was it for G.I. Joe's advertising, until at least the late 1960s. The first large ad I found where G.I. Joe's probably would have paid most of the ad's cost, ran in 1970 for garden and lawn products. I did see the store name mentioned in ads run in *The Oregonian* for a product prior to that. But the ad just mentioned the product could be found at G.I. Joe's, and I am assuming the manufacturer ran the ad and not the store.

Of course, G.I. Joe's did start advertising regularly, especially when the chain included stores in multiple locations. Display ads eventually appeared in the newspaper, along with special newspaper inserts, and radio and TV ads.

But in the early days, Dad depended on word-of-mouth promotion and on the North Portland store's great location, so close to the Washington/Oregon Interstate Bridge.

Dad also had a great sense of responsibility, not only for his family, but also for his employees. My brother and I were talking about this recently and I learned something I found amazing. David told me that in 1965, Dad invited the Retail Clerks Union to talk to employees about unionizing because he wanted employees to have good health benefits, which would be available through the union. At that time, there was just one store location, and there were not enough employees to get a good insurance plan through the business. While this move was in the best interests of his employees, I wonder how many other bosses would have invited in the union.

Dad started an employee stock purchase plan, too, after G.I.

Joe's incorporated in the early 1960s. I can remember him talking about how he wanted to share the success of the company with those who helped make it happen.

David has suggested to me that Dad's feeling of responsibility could have originated while he was serving as a bomber pilot in World War II. First, he wanted to contribute to a victory in the war, which any member of the armed services would have wanted to do. Then, he also had the responsibility of completing his bombing missions, in order to aid our forces on the ground and at sea.

But there was a level of more personal responsibility, as well. David thinks that, as a B-24 bomber pilot, Dad felt keenly responsible for the lives of his 10 crew members. It was his job to get them to their target and then back to the base safely. This must have been a heavy weight.

Dad's promotion to squadron leader meant that the safety of the crews of the nine other planes in the squadron became his responsibility, too. And with his promotion to group squadron leader, that responsibility was again multiplied.

Dad must have carried that feeling of responsibility for the people he worked with when he eventually moved from the Army Air Forces to G.I. Joe's.

Finally, I believe an essential basis for the store's success grew from Dad's appreciation of nature and the outdoors. He grew up in Hoquiam, Washington, surrounded by the magnificent moderate-rain forest of the Pacific Northwest, even though it was being logged in the area when he was growing up. Hoquiam was situated at Grays Harbor, so the ocean was part of this childhood, as well.

His maternal grandfather had a cabin on Hood's Canal where

Exterior wall with map of the Columbia Gorge and Mt. Hood National Forest. Photo from article in 1973 The Sporting Goods Retailer. *Used with permission of publisher, SportsOneSource, LLC.*

the family would spend summers. They would go clamming for the abundant butter clams or wait for the shrimp boat to come by, with fresh-caught shrimp to sell. (Unfortunately, the family lost the cabin in the Great Depression, due to unpaid property taxes.)

As an adult, Dad was too focused on his business to hunt or fish like so many of his customers did, but he did enjoy boating in a ski boat on the Columbia River. He also liked to hike. First the whole family, and then just Dad and I, would often hike the five-mile trail loop from Multnomah Falls to Wahkeena Falls in the Columbia Gorge just east of Portland. We hiked on occasional Sundays, from 1960 through 1962. Also that is when I wanted to practice freeway driving with my new driver's license, and Dad patiently let me do the driving to the falls.

G.I. Joe's relationship with the outdoors was displayed in the early 1970s on an outside wall of the Rockwood store. A huge map of the Columbia Gorge, along with a smaller one of the

Mt. Hood National Forest, dominated the wall in front of the parking lot. The business slogan at that time was, "The Outdoor World of G.I. Joe's."

Looking back, I can see Dad had many qualities that helped him create G.I. Joe's. He also knew that it was possible for him to start his own business, because he had seen his father, mother, and brothers do just that. He had the constant, invaluable support of my mother, Charmian Orkney. These personal qualities, knowledge, and family support made it possible for him to weather several start-ups and many setbacks, until he and G.I. Joe's were successful.

But I also think that G.I. Joe's was successful because it offered products that people in the Pacific Northwest wanted. So many people in Oregon and Washington, then and now, love to be outdoors, whether they are hiking, camping, fishing, hunting, rafting, or skiing. The original army surplus store stocked merchandise that made these activities easier and more enjoyable for folks. This merchandise included sleeping bags, cots, tents, boots, knapsacks, and rafts, which were the forerunners of today's recreational sporting goods.

Dad's lifelong appreciation of nature helped him to see how these G.I. surplus goods would be popular in the Pacific Northwest.

I also think that Dad's modesty matched a basic trait of people living in the top left corner of the United States, which helped make his presentation of the store attractive to his customers. He did not advertise in the early days; customers had to find G.I. Joe's on their own. The store layout was not fancy, and the merchandise was not displayed in a flashy manner. Also, employees were not pushy, so customers could look around the store for as long as they wanted, just like the sign at the store entrance invited them to. ▪

Growing up with G.I. Joe's

Chapter 30

A Realization

*Dad and me in Riverside, California,
where he was serving in the Army Air Forces in 1945.*

A while back, I was hit with the realization that I missed my dad! I know it sounds pretty basic to miss a deceased parent, but I thought that I had dealt with his loss since he had passed away so many years ago. I believed that every time there was a mention of G.I. Joe's, I became sad because the store was no more.

While that was true, the deeper part of missing G.I. Joe's was because it was like an extension of my father. After his passing, I was still able to stop by a store and feel his influence. So much of Dad's outlook on life was evident in the way he ran G.I. Joe's. And after he died, I believe that most of the business practices continued on during the years that my brother was CEO and board chairman.

I would sum up my dad's approach as fairness based on merit, with store operations as basic and simple as possible.

His "no frills" philosophy was evident in the design of stores and with his office. As mentioned previously, the early store additions and then expansion stores were concrete tilt-up, similar to warehouses, and the fixtures were often built in-house. In the 1970s, his office was in a large room next to the loading dock of Store 1, where Barbara Mallery and her accounting staff had their desks, as well. Large windows in the office looked out to the stock receiving and shipping area. How many other CEOs can you think of who share such a simple, group office?

Dad's fairness with employees and customers was demonstrated in many stories I heard from my brother. Here is one. Dad loaned money to an employee in the early 1970s so he could buy a reliable car to get to work on time.

According to David, when the employee arrived late one morning to the Oak Grove store because he had been unable to get his car started, Dad happened to be in that store. After Dad heard the story, he handed the employee some cash and told him to buy a car and to pay back the money when he could. The employee did indeed buy a car and did pay Dad back. And he continued working for G.I. Joe's and went on into management.

When David became CEO in late 1976, he continued with

Dad's grounded-in-simplicity approach. For instance, it was not until 1982 that the company's administrative office was moved to the newly-built facility in Wilsonville. And that only happened because the company did not renew their lease on the Store 1 building, where the offices were, because the nearby Delta Park store had opened in North Portland and replaced the old store.

So, until 1982, all the central offices for the business were located in the second-floor addition of the first G.I. Joe's store at 8700 N. Vancouver Avenue. These were very basic offices where buyers saw vendors and placed orders, and all the folks in other administrative departments worked as well, including operations, accounting, marketing, and information technology.

The offices were small and windowless, and saying they were not fancy is putting it mildly. To get to the offices, you had to walk up a wide stairway from the loading dock which had a large conveyor belt on one side of it. While the conveyor belt did seem out of place there, it was helpful to use if you had something heavy to bring up the stairs, as vendors often did.

Although the administrative offices were basic back then, I never heard grumbling about them when I worked as Box Office manager. There was too much work to do to spare any time for thinking about the office situation! Besides, everybody working so closely together really aided in inter-department communication and friendliness, which was a good thing for the business, I think.

I'll just bet it was quite an adjustment for those moving from the old offices to the new ones, and I wouldn't be surprised if there wasn't just a little nostalgia for the old place. Of course, that is just a guess on my part!

In 1998, David sold out to Norm Daniels and his financial

partners. By then, I no longer lived in Portland, and I stopped by a store only when I was on a trip up from Southern California to visit family members. While I no longer felt like a part of the new G.I. Joe's, I could still feel Dad's influence, somewhat, when I did visit. Like I said, the store always felt like a sibling of David's and mine, and now it felt like one that had been adopted by someone we knew and was still the same in many ways.

However, any remaining feeling of closeness to the store evaporated when G.I. Joe's morphed into Joe's Sports, Outdoor and More in 2007. I did not go in any of the stores from that time until the liquidation in 2009. I knew it would have been too much of a challenge for me to see the "improvements" to the store, if the new management's choice of new name for the chain was any indication of their business judgment!

Fast forward to March 19, 2013, when I read a story in *The Oregonian* that mentioned G.I. Joe's. I felt the familiar sadness hit me. Then I realized I was missing Dad. As long as the store was still open in some form, it felt to me like some part of him was still there for customers, employees and family. That final link to Dad was broken with the liquidation of Joe's Sports, Outdoor and More.

When I started writing this story in 2008, I wanted not only to tell Dad's story, but also to talk about the ideals on which he founded G.I. Joe's. I think these ideals were a huge part of the success of the business in the early years, and I think they are still relevant today.

But in 2008, the company was not recognizing any of Dad's contributions to the business. The official company website around that time dismissed him as a "clever pilot" who had left a small but thriving business when he died in 1976. To me, *clever* did not describe Dad, who was quiet and deeply intelligent. And to me, *small* did not describe a business that grossed $34 million in sales in the year of his death.

The website description was a way of making Dad "less than," so that current management would look better. I felt it was only a matter of time till his name was erased from the story of G.I. Joe's.

I did not want that to happen. ■

Growing up with G.I. Joe's

Chapter 31

It's a Wrap

David and I taking a break from a
backyard croquet game in Portland in 1949.

Today it is just my brother, David, and me who remain from the family members gathered around the dinner table in the early 1950s, discussing how well tarpaulins were selling in the North Portland G.I. Joe's.

As I finish writing my history in 2015, David lives in

Portland, and I live in Southern California to be nearer my children and their families.

In writing this history, I have referred to my brother by his given name, David, even though I always think of him by his Orkney family nickname of Corky.

I have been known by more than one name, too. When I was growing up, I was known as Jan Orkney. In the Portland area, from 1978 to around 1990, I was known as Jan Nizam, which was my married name with a shortened first name. Also, my advertising and public relations business in Lake Oswego in the mid-1980s was named Nizam Media.

When I went back to using my original name, Orkney, around 1990, I started using my full first name, Janna.

It was a challenge to decide what photos to include in *Growing Up With G.I. Joe's*. First, I chose some family photos that David and I had kept over the years. Then, David shared with me many photos of G.I. Joe's stores, both inside and out from later years that appear in these pages.

I also had photos from my mother's family that I included in the book and I received some early Orkney family photos from my cousin, Mary Lynn Orkney Conlon, as well. From the lack of photos of G.I. Joe's in the early days, it is obvious that Dad and Mom did not take many photos of the store. Now, everyone seems to carry a smart-phone and snap pictures at a moment's notice, but when I was young, picture-taking was reserved for special occasions.

So there were photos of David and me taken every Easter Sunday when we were kids, but no pictures of us ever taken inside or outside of G.I. Joe's as children or young adults. I guess there was no special occasion to memorialize there. And for that

David and I at Pioneer Square in downtown Portland in June, 2014.

matter, there were no pictures taken of Dad or Mom in or out of the store, either, when I was growing up.

Another possible reason for the lack of photos of the early store is that my parents were just too busy living life to think of making a photographic record of what they were doing.

The other realization that came to me as I sorted through images was that Mom was the photographer in our family. The small number of photos taken in my childhood seldom included Mom because she was behind the camera. I wish there had been more.

I realize that I may have given the impression by the way I wrote the book that the four or five of us, if you count G.I. Joe's as a sibling, were an ideal family that always got along peacefully with each other. Of course, there is no such thing as an ideal family, and we certainly had our share of disagreements. However, at this point in my life, I am happy to let those go and focus on what was good and life-affirming in the family. That was my focus while writing *Growing Up With G.I. Joe's*.

I also realize that after finishing this book, a reader might assume that I am wealthy because of all the money G.I. Joe's took in over the years. That would be nice, but I am not.

For compelling reasons, it became a good decision for me to sell all my stock in the store in the early 1980s, before Dad's estate closed. I did just that and so did not participate financially in the continued growth of the store.

At the time, it was hard to let go of that link to the family business. However, I am happy to say that eventually I moved on and have thrived elsewhere. I was able to discover my strengths, interests, and talents and learn how I could contribute to my larger community, apart from G.I. Joe's.

So today, life IS good and I am happy. With that wrap-up, I will end my story. I have enjoyed writing it, gathering the photos, and thinking back to when I was growing up with G.I. Joe's.

I hope you have enjoyed reading the book and that it has stirred up some of your own memories, as well.

In looking back to those early days of G.I. Joe's, I marvel at the store's contribution to life and recreation in the Pacific Northwest, and commend all the people who helped make it happen. I also marvel at the simple beginnings that preceded the store, when Dad sold sleeping bags on street corners in Portland, and at his incredible determination to build a business from that.

It is still hard for me to accept that after all the years when so many people worked so hard to build and grow G.I. Joe's, the new management stumbled and the store went bankrupt in

2009, so quickly after they took over the business. Wouldn't it be wonderful if G.I. Joe's continued on today, outfitting folks in Oregon, Washington and Idaho, so that we could go have fun in the great outdoors?

Well, for over 50 years, G.I. Joe's did just that! The sign on the side of the first building on North Vancouver Avenue read, "Come in and browse around," and a lot of people did, and a lot of them found what they needed to get outside. Other stores are outfitting people of the Pacific Northwest today, but G.I. Joe's built that foundation. I am very grateful to have been around to see it happen. ▪

Growing up with G.I. Joe's

G.I. Joe's Timeline

1948   G.I. Joe's war surplus store in North Portland started by six partners, including Edward Orkney

1952   Edward Orkney took over G.I. Joe's as sole owner

1950s   Store changed from a G.I. tent to larger and larger wood frame buildings through upgrades and additions

1955   G.I. Joe's joined Worldwide Distributors, Seattle-based buying cooperative

1960   Store doubled footage with concrete tilt-up addition

1966   Store 2 built next to original store featuring sports and auto merchandise

1968   Store 3 built at same North Portland location, featuring hardware, crafts and do-it-yourself merchandise

1970   First branch store opened in Rockwood, between Portland and Gresham, Oregon
G.I. Joe's stopped selling cigarettes

1972   Second branch store opened southeast of Portland in Oak Grove

1974   Third branch store opened at Beaverton Mall in Beaverton, Oregon, and was the first store in a large shopping center

1975   David Orkney opened first Jean Machine store in Beaverton Mall

1976	The fourth branch and fifth location for G.I. Joe's opened in Salem, Oregon, and was the first store outside the Portland Metro area.
	Founder Edward Orkney died in December
	David Orkney became CEO of G.I. Joe's
1978	Construction began on Distribution center in Wilsonville, Oregon
1979	The Box Office ticket outlet system opened in all Portland area stores
	New Distribution Center opened in Wilsonville.
	G.I. Joe's opened at a sixth location in Eastport Plaza in southeast Portland
	The second out-of-Portland store opened in Bend, Oregon
1981	Seven G.I. Joe's locations and 16 Jean Machine Stores posted $68 million in sales in FY 1981
1982	Delta Park store opened in North Portland, replacing the original store and stores Number 2 and 3 that closed
	New administrative and buying office was built in Wilsonville next to distribution center and management moved in
1983	G.I. Joe's store opened in Eugene, Oregon
	Jean Machine operated at least 15 stores in Oregon and Washington
1985	Tualatin, Oregon, store opened
	Second Salem store opened in South Salem
1986	Medford, Oregon, store opened
	Distribution Center in Wilsonville expanded

1987	Gresham, Oregon, store opened, replacing first branch store, Rockwood, which closed and Fred Meyer bought the property for addition to their store across street Ticketmaster System opened in Portland area G.I. Joe's stores plus in Jean Machine at Galleria in downtown Portland
1989	First store opened in Washington state in Vancouver, close to the I-205 Freeway Albany, Oregon, store opened
1990	A total of 13 G.I. Joe's stores total, with one store in Washington and 12 in Oregon All remaining Jean Machine Stores sold between January 31, 1989 and January 31, 1990, since none were listed in 1990 financial statement
1991	The second Washington store opened in Federal Way, north of Tacoma with new focus on sports and automotive merchandise
1992	David Orkney handed over CEO duties to Norm Daniels and continued as chairman of the board. There were 14 G.I. Joe's stores.
1996	Store in Issaquah, Washington, opened
1997	Opening of store in Puyallup, Washington
May 1998	Norm Daniels and financial partners bought out David Orkney and became new owners of G.I. Joe's Hillsboro, Oregon, store opened
1999	Store in Lynnwood, Washington, opened
2001	Store in Sherwood, Oregon, opened

2002	Stores opened in both Lakewood and Kent, Washington
2003	G.I. Joe's first urban core store opened in Seattle, Washington, in the Northgate Mall
2004	Johnson Creek, Oregon, store opened and replaced Eastport Plaza store in southeast Portland area Opening of Lake Stevens, Washington, store
2005	Mt. Vernon, Washington, store opened (23rd store)
2006	Kennewick, Washington, store in Tri-Cities area opened South Salem store changed to outlet store. Bellingham, Washington, branch opened
2007	Gryphon Investors of San Francisco bought out Norm Daniels and partners. Daniels remained as CEO Store name changed to Joe's Sports, Outdoor and More Kirkland and Bellevue, Washington, stores opened, but Bellevue closed by mid-2008 First store in Idaho opened in Meridian Opening of Spokane Valley, Washington, store
2008	Hal Smith, formerly of Pro Bass Shops, became CEO, replacing Norm Daniels Second Idaho store opened in Nampa Renton, Washington, store opened Made total of 31 Joe's Sports, Outdoor and More stores
March 2009	Joe's Sports, Outdoor and More filed for bankruptcy
April 2009	Liquidation sale began in all stores ▪

Joe's Sports, Outdoor and More 2009 Store Locations

T here were 31 stores in the chain, located in Idaho, Oregon and Washington, when G.I. Joe's successor store, Joe's Sports, Outdoor and More, filed for bankruptcy in March 2009. It was then owned by San Francisco-based Gryphon Investors.

Idaho Store Locations
Meridian

Nampa

Oregon Store Locations
Albany

Beaverton

Bend

Delta Park (Portland)

Eugene

Gresham

Hillsboro

Johnson Creek (Portland)

Medford

Oak Grove

Salem

Sherwood

South Salem

Tualatin

Washington Store Locations

Bellingham

Federal Way

Issaquah

Kennewick

Kent

Kirkland

Lake Stevens

Lakewood

Lynnwood

Mt. Vernon

Puyallup

Renton

Seattle

Spokane Valley

Vancouver

G.I. Joe's, Inc. Employee Share Program (ESP) Gross Sales Sharing

I am sure we have all heard of companies' profit sharing plans for employees, but have you ever heard of a company giving employees a share of its gross sales? Well G.I. Joe's did. My dad, Ed Orkney, started a gross sales sharing program in 1968, and this says more to me about his business philosophy and concern for his employees than anything else I can think of. That is why I am adding it to *Growing Up With G.I. Joe's* as an addendum, now in May 2015, even though I have already completed the book.

You see, I only found the Employee Share Program description a few months ago. It was attached to an old letter from Dad that was stuck in a file folder. The letter, dated October 17, 1968, was written to my husband and I when we were living in Southern California. Dad's letter was easy to read but the attached paper describing the ESP was almost illegible. It had been mimeographed and the text had faded so much that I could hardly read the words.

After much effort, I succeeded in deciphering the faded words by making photo copies of the page over and over, using the dark exposure setting. When I was finally able to read Dad's plan that gave employees a share of gross merchandise sales, I was amazed! Why hadn't I remembered reading about this in 1968? I guess I just did not note its significance then but I do now, and that is why I want to share it with you.

First, let's place the plan in perspective by quoting from my dad's October 17, 1968, letter:

> *Well we have had the new store (Store 3) open for two days now and it looks like it will be alright. We have 16,000 ft. of toys displayed and I think it is the largest display anywhere. Anyway it is a lot of fun.*

Dad mentioned later in the letter that G.I. Joe's had 160 employees at the time.

Now here is the deciphered ESP program sheet. From Dad's introductory remarks, I am guessing that my husband and I were sent a copy of an information page that was being sent to other members of Worldwide Distributors, then in Seattle, Washington. Here is the text:

> *Special Share Program*
> *To Members only:*
>
> *Dear (name illegible): Would you please publish our Employee Share Program and eligibility requirements, both of which are enclosed. We have had enthusiastic response among employees and some quite controversial opinions among other store owners. Regardless, it should be of interest to any store owner and they should bear in mind that we had a similar and larger percentage plan among supervisory*

personnel for fifteen years. This ESP is merely an extension of a present plan to more employees.

—Ed Orkney

Commencing September 1st, 1968, G.I. Joe's, Inc. will institute a trial employee share program (ESP). This plan will be based on a percentage of the sales as a bonus. Those eligible will be all full time employees (other than supervisory personnel) who have been continually employed at G.I. Joe's for six months or longer. We estimate that approximately 50 employees will be immediately eligible.

How it works: Every two months G.I. Joe's would divide one half of one percent of the gross merchandise sales of all three stores, less employee charges, (and less) Prestone and other loss leader sales among ESP participants. For example, if the sales for the September and October period are one million dollars, one half percent is $5,000.00. If there are fifty people, each one would receive an ESP check for $100.00 less the usual tax deductions.

This plan may be withdrawn at the end of any two months period. It is not intended to be made a part of any union contract or negotiation and is not an attempt to harm the union's bargaining position in any way.

Frankly, it is an experiment on the part of management in an effort to bring most personnel into more direct sharing of the success of G.I. Joe's. If it produces more enthusiasm, alertness and efficiency on

*the part of the employees and thus results in more
sales and profits it will more than likely be increased.
If it lays an egg, it will be dropped. Speaking bluntly,
it is up to you to make it work and to make G.I. Joe's
wish to augment it. It is a bold plan as it is based on
gross sales rather than net profit. We think it will
work and some day be increased.*

*To keep you informed, a running total of sales will
be posted daily. If you have any questions, consult
your department head.*

(The text went on to describe in detail how the plan would
work.) ▮

Acknowledgements

I first wrote about G.I. Joe's in 1980 in a paper required for a History of Portland class. I took the class at Portland State University and it was taught by noted Portland historian, Dr. Kimbark MacColl. My paper, titled, "Ed Orkney and G.I. Joe's," was a 16-page history of Dad and the store up to that time. I enjoyed the class, and, incidentally, got an "A" on the paper.

To gather material for the paper, I formally interviewed my mother and brother individually in October 1980. I also interviewed G.I. Joe's Vice President, Norm Daniels, that November.

In addition, I read two articles from national business magazines, copies of which my dad had sent to me when I lived in Southern California. (He had been so proud that G.I. Joe's got national coverage!)

One article was in the March 20, 1973 issue of *Camping Industry Magazine*, titled, "A Big Volume Specialty Retailer, and was a 2-page spread. The other article was from the December 1973 *Sporting Goods Dealer Magazine*, and was titled "Spawned in Tent, Oregonian to Chalk Up $4 Million in '73," pages 87-90.

Rounding out my research, I read a newspaper article about G.I. Joe's from the August 28, 1980, *Vaughn Street Journal*.

In 2008, the idea came to me to write an updated history of G.I. Joe's and post it on the internet in blog form, so that readers could make comments. It took me three or four months of writing and I recall that the history was made up of about 5 short chapters. When I finished in July of that year, I managed to put the chapters up on Blogspot, the free blog format offered by Google.

It was heartwarming to me to receive comments on the blog, both from folks I knew and those that were new to me.

Then, in March 2009, Joe's Sports, Outdoor and More declared bankruptcy. My website received a lot of hits during that sad time, especially after I posted a link to it on one of the threads on **www.IFish.net**. I so appreciate the website's creator Jennie Logsdon-Martin for allowing me to post there. And I appreciate the many members who commented on my IFish.net posts or sent me emails.

I kept the G.I. Joe's history online for about three years, until I decided to take the blog story and turn it into a book. So, I removed the information from Blogspot and started the long process of adding and transforming chapters.

In the early months of writing the book I drew mostly on what I remembered, augmented with information from innumerable phone conversations with my brother, David, and my mother's sister, Joey Stout Hadfield. They were both profoundly helpful, willing to answer innumerable questions from me, and I am so grateful.

My two cousins, Bruce Orkney and Mary Lynn Conlon Orkney also aided me. They both shared a lot of information about family history, including some writings by our uncle, Syd Orkney. I incorporated much of this information into the book. And as mentioned in the wrap up, Mary Lynn provided a lot of family photos as well, many of which appear on these pages.

Then, in the summer of 2013, I came to the decision that it was time to pick up the phone and talk to people I didn't know. I wanted to gain a perspective on how G.I. Joe's fit into the larger picture of general retail in the Pacific Northwest, with particular emphasis on those stores that started out by selling war surplus after World War II.

This was a big step for me. Cold calling to try to get an interview for the book seemed daunting, until I made the first call to Worldwide Distributors in Kent, Washington.

I was put right through to President Mark Williams, and he was so amicable and helpful, that my anxieties dissolved. Mark answered my questions and talked about Worldwide's early days. He sent me Worldwide's 50th anniversary newsletter that had a long article about the founding of the buying group and profiles of early members, including G.I. Joe's. He also sent some photos of David and G.I. Joe's that appear in the book.

Mark Williams suggested I call Charles Grigg of Griggs Department Store in Washington's Tri-Cities. Charles and his store were early members of Worldwide. Again, cold-calling one of the Griggs stores, I first talked with Charles' son, Charlie. He was friendly and shared information, and remembered my brother. Then, I was able to talk to Charles, and portions of our conversation appear in *Growing Up With G.I. Joe's*.

As related in the book, it was a very strong suggestion from Charles Grigg that led me to call Bob's Sporting Goods in Longview, Washington, to try to connect with founder Bob Schlecht. I left a phone message for him and Bob so graciously called me back. As one of Worldwide's founders, he shared stories with me on the buying co-op's beginnings and also about Dad. Again, the information is in the book.

I also made a special trip to Portland in October 2013 to look through G.I. Joe's and family photos with David, but mainly to go with him to Longview to meet Bob, Sr.; Bob, Jr., or Bobby; and grandson Matt, who now runs the store.

That meeting was very moving for me and my brother, too. Bob Schlecht just seems to radiate love and goodwill, and it felt so good to meet him! We also had an enjoyable time visiting with Bob, Bobby, and Matt over lunch. Bob even gave us a lesson in the easy way to get catsup to start pouring out of a bottle. Now I know! And here's a hint: the method does not include sticking a knife into the bottle, as I have been known to do on occasion.

To find out about the Yard Birds store in Chehalis, a founding and trend-setting member of Worldwide, and about owners Rich Gillingham and Bill Jones, I went to the website, **www.yardbirdshistory.com**. I also bought and watched the interesting, DVD, "Skinny and Fatty, the story of Yard Birds," by Port Northwest. In addition, I talked on the phone to Tom Sturza, son-in-law of co-founder, Rich Gillingham.

During my October 2013 Portland visit, I stopped by the Oregon Historical Society to search their archives for photos of the Vanport Flood. To find more flood photos, I then contacted Thomas Robinson of the Historical Photo Archive when I returned home.

Tom's and my conversations and his extensive knowledge of Portland history led to the discovery of new photos and information about G.I. Joe's early days. I am very thankful to him for helping make *Growing Up With G.I. Joe's* a more complete book.

As the scope of the book enlarged, I turned again to my brother for information and stories on G.I. Joe's expansion and the folks responsible for it. David was always ready to answer a quick question, or elaborate on a topic to help the history come alive to me. A huge "thank you" to my brother! This book would have been much, much less without his tremendous input.

In addition to talks with my brother, a print resource on the store in the early 1990s was an article in the national magazine, *Discount Merchandiser*, in the January 1992 issue, pages 22 to 28. It was titled, "G.I. Joe's: Exploiting a Niche," with a subtitle of "Mass merchant niche retailer G.I. Joe's, a 14-store Oregon chain, reveals how modifications helped its latest store adapt to the Seattle Market."

I also turned to *The Oregonian Archives* to fact-check my information and dates as much as possible. For facts and opinion written after 1987, I went directly to **www.OregonLive.com**. For anything written or featured in the paper prior to 1987, I looked at The Multnomah County Library's *Historical Oregonian Archive*. What a valuable resource! That was where I found all the information about the newspaper advertising of Portland-area war surplus stores in the late 1940s and early 1950s.

I also want to thank Fred Rau for mentioning the baby pheasant story to me, in the hope that it would be part of the history. It is. And I am grateful to schoolmates Lana Blomgren Miller and Kathy McCuddy Johnson for relating what happened when the Columbia River flooded their backyards… Lana for sharing memories of the Vanport Flood in 1948 and Kathy for her memories of the flood threat of 1956.

Finally, I want to thank so many others who encouraged me in writing this history. When my energy or enthusiasm would start to lag, invariably someone would happen to ask how *Growing Up* was progressing, and that would get me motivated again to keep on writing.

Thank you all so much! And thanks to book designer Susan Wells for her book cover design and book interior which I love and to copy editor Tammy Ditmore, who showed me how to make the story flow more easily in so many places. I also appreciate the diligence of proofreaders Linda M. Stern, Kathy M. Johnson, and Fred Rau. Their comments were invaluable in helping me correct mistakes and rein in my use of commas.

And now, I push back my chair from the computer keyboard. I am finished writing the history of G.I. Joe's and my family and the time of my growing up in mid 20th century Portland.

I can relax now and send the book out in the world, letting it tell the story of that special time and place. ■

Index

Christmas 1966, 77

Columbia Avenue home/neighborhood, 27-28, 43-49, 51, 63, 166

Disneyland trip, 1956, 58-59

high school graduations, 73

Janna's wedding, 74

Jantzen Beach Amusement Park trips, 48

Mission San Juan Capistrano trip, 1956, 59-60

move to Portland suburbs, 63-65

Russet Street house, 6

Sacramento Street house, 63, 65

Tarps (dog), 29, 44

Pacific Hardware and Electric Company (Portland, OR), 9

Pacific Northwest stores, 114

Pant Shop, The, 80

Pasco, Washington, 139, 144

Patterson, Barbara, 111

Pearl Harbor, Japanese bombing of, 35, 170

Pioneer Square (Portland, OR), 191

Port Angeles, Washington, 144

Port Townsend, Washington, 169, 170

Portland, Oregon, 1, 3, 6, 7, 9, 10, 19, 20, 22, 23, 31, 63, 73, 74, 75, 76, 77, 80, 82, 83, 84, 106, 107, 111, 125, 141, 144, 145, 148, 180, 186, 189, 191

    area, 2, 4, 81, 89, 96, 105, 119, 114, 190

    East, 3, 98

    North, 1, 2, 3, 6, 7, 19, 22, 60, 69, 75, 76, 77, 80, 82, 89, 94, 95, 97, 101, 107, 111, 133, 136, 143, 146, 152, 178, 185

    southeast, 19, 20, 89, 107

    See also specific G.I. Joe's stores

Portland Airport, 48

Portland Civic Stadium and Auditorium, 106, 107

Portland Expo Center, 132

Portland Housing Authority, 10

Growing up with G.I. Joe's

About the Author

Janna Orkney's heart belongs in the Pacific Northwest and she doesn't think it is an accident that she and Oregon share the same birthday. She was born in Aberdeen, Washington, and she and her family lived in Hoquiam and Seattle, Washington, and Salem, Oregon, before settling in Portland in 1948.

As an adult, Janna lived in the Portland area for a number of years, where she provided public relations and advertising services to companies and events through her business, Nizam Media, in Lake Oswego.

Today, Janna lives in Southern California to be near her three grown children and their families. In the author's spare time, she enjoys serving as an elected member of the board of directors of her local water and wastewater treatment agency, playing with her grandchildren, and heading for the beach in all kinds of weather.

Janna says that she feels blessed to have grown up in the Pacific Northwest. ■

Please Share Your G.I. Joe's Stories and Photos

Do you have a story about G.I. Joe's or a photo of one of the stores or G.I. Joe's promotional products that you would like to share? Please send them to me!

I would love to publish your stories or photos in a booklet that I plan to assemble after the book is published. I then can offer the booklet for sale at the **www.GrowingUpWithGIjoes.com** website. However, if I do not receive enough material to make a booklet, I can put it online at the website.

For your information, I will include only the contributor's name and city with the story or photo, but NO other personal information, like street address, email address, or phone number, and will not share your personal information with any other person or entity.

So please email your stories to **theGIJoesStory@gmail.com**. If you attach photos, please include the name of the photographers, a description of the subjects, and approximate dates they were taken.

After I receive your stories and photos, I will email a form for you to sign and return to me that would allow me to publish what you sent.

Any questions? You can email me at: **theGIJoesStory@gmail.com**.

Thank you in advance for your response! Don't think about it, just go for it! ■

Janna Orkney

To Order Books Online

www.GrowingUpWithGIJoes.com

This is where to go to order the book online directly from the author, Janna Orkney. You can also check out:

- Possible books related to *Growing Up With G.I. Joe's* by the author or others.
- The booklet or online e-book containing readers' stories and photos of G.I. Joe's (when it is completed)
- Special offers of non-book items

At the website, you can also follow Janna's book promotion event schedule and find links to articles and other media mention of *Growing Up With G.I. Joe's*.

To contact the author, send an email to: **GrowingUpWithGIJoes22@gmail.com**. Janna is available for presentations about the book and for selling books as a fundraiser for your organization.

You are invited to visit the Growing Up With G.I. Joe's Facebook page (please "Like" it), and to follow Janna on Twitter **@JannaAuthor**